Welcome

Family history – genealogy – is one of the fastest growing hobbies in Britain. Over the past thirty years looking for one's ancestors has become an immensely popular pastime – perhaps a million people across the UK are now trying to piece together their family tree.

And of course, we have all been moved by the stories revealed in the *Who Do You Think You Are* TV series. However, our ancestors are every bit as interesting as those of the celebrities who appear in the shows. On my family tree alone I have found merchant navy officers, victims of the Nazis, generations of Leicestershire vicars as well as a secretive London wine merchant. I've not found anybody remotely famous or even rich, but it doesn't matter.

In part, this explosion of interest is due to the internet, and to excellent online resources which allow subscribers to easily do the same research from their armchairs which even a decade ago might have taken them months or not have been possible at all.

But for me and many others the real thrill lies in visiting archives – there are hundreds, large and small, scattered across the British Isles – and reading documents which may have been handled by your ancestors, and possibly even signed by them. There is nothing else which quite compares to that. And even if you can't find anything written by them, you may well get a buzz visiting the village, perhaps even the house, they came from.

The great thing about family history is that it is a hobby that you can pick up or put down when it suits you. After all, your ancestors are not going to disappear. There is no pressure to trace everybody you are descended from – indeed it is nearly impossible. Most people only research one side of their family or a few ancestors who particularly interest them. And if one forebear is frustratingly elusive, well there are always plenty of others out there for you to find.

Another wonderful aspect of the pastime is how friendly and helpful most family historians are. If you get lost on your first visit to a record office, the chance is that somebody will be only too pleased to point you in the right direction. Genealogists are a very sociable lot, and you will receive a warm welcome at a local family history society meeting or adult education class. Another place to share information are the online mailing lists, dedicated to almost every aspect of family history search.

For some, family history leads them into totally new directions. One friend of mine has become the world expert in William Cuffey – the 19th century black Chartist leader, while another has become fascinated with the history of paper – all he wanted to do was to find out what his great-grandfather, a paper glazer, did.

So don't say I didn't warn you if genealogy takes over your life completely!

Simon Fowler

About *Ancestors*

I hope you will enjoy this magazine and find it useful in your research. It contains a variety of articles of the sort which appear in every issue of *Ancestors* magazine, which is on sale at W H Smiths every month. Better still, why not subscribe and receive it before it reaches the shops and save 15 per cent off the cover price. For details see page 92.

EDITOR

SIMON FOWLER
ANCESTORS
THE NATIONAL ARCHIVES
RUSKIN AVENUE
KEW
RICHMOND
TW9 4DU
TEL: 020 8392 5370
FAX: 020 8487 1974
EMAIL: ancestors@nationalarchives.gov.uk

EDITORIAL ASSISTANCE

PENNY LAW / PAUL WILKINSON / SANDRA GRANT

ADVERTISING MANAGER

CAROLYN MILLS
TEL: 01226 734704
FAX: 01226 734703
EMAIL: carolynm@whmagazines.co.uk

DESIGN

PAUL WILKINSON
EMAIL: design@pen-and-sword.co.uk

PRINTERS

WARNERS (MIDLANDS) PLC

PUBLISHED BY

THE NATIONAL ARCHIVES
KEW
RICHMOND
SURREY
TW9 4DU

WHARNCLIFFE PUBLISHING LTD
THE DRILL HALL, EASTGATE
BARNSLEY
SOUTH YORKSHIRE S70 2EU

CONTENTS

GETTING STARTED

6 First steps

There's never been a better time to start researching your family history. MARGARET WARD shows you where and how to begin.

10 Looking up your lineage online

Many resources needed by beginners are just the click of a mouse away. PETER CHRISTIAN guides you through the most useful websites.

12 Certificates

Births, marriage and death certificates are key resources. We look at getting the most out of them.

16 Making sense of the census

Every 10 years the government takes a census which should tell us who lived where on one particular evening. SIMON FOWLER enumerates what you might find in these vital records.

20 Benefit from a will

Whether your ancestors owned large swathes of land or came from a more humble background, the chances are that a few left behind wills. DAVID ANNAL reads through them.

USING THE NATIONAL ARCHIVES

28 Making the best use of Kew

In the course of your family history researches, you are almost certain to use the records held by The National Archives. SIMON FOWLER offers some advice about getting the most out of your visit.

30 The New Kew

Using our step-by-step guide, PENNY LAW takes you through the reading rooms.

34 Who, where and when

MELINDA HAUNTON explains how the National Register of Archives can help family historians track down where records are held.

THE CELTIC CONNECTION

38 Trace your Irish ancestors

Start researching your family in Ireland as IAN MAXWELL takes you on a journey through the basic record sources.

42 Researching the Scots

DAVID McVEY considers the sources for finding Scottish ancestors online.

Subscribe to *Ancestors* and save up to **15%** off cover price See page 92

MILITARY RECORDS

46 Before 1913
During the 18th and 19th centuries tens of thousands of men served in the British Army and Royal Navy. SIMON FOWLER looks through their records.

50 The First World War
The First World War affected virtually every family in the United Kingdom. MICHAEL PATERSON shows you how to trace ancestors who served.

58 Medals and the family historian
JOHN SLY says that medals can be an informative source of information as well as being a splendid link with our forebears.

EARLY RECORDS

64 Parish registers
Parish registers are an invaluable resource, particularly before 1837. ANTHONY ADOLPH finds out more.

68 Nonconformist records
MICHAEL GANDY says it is important to understand what shaped our ancestors' choices and beliefs.

72 Insightful inscriptions
There is a wealth of genealogical information in local graveyards. RICHARD SMART discovers why.

HELPFUL ADVICE

76 Why can't I find them?
Don't be downhearted when you seem to have reached the end of the line in your researches. MICHAEL GANDY suggests ways around the brick wall.

80 Preserving pictures and papers
LESLIE CRAM explains how he archived some 4,000 family photographs, along with notes, diaries, letters and other documents.

84 Here to help
Family history is a sociable hobby. We suggest organisations and societies who can provide advice and a chance to meet fellow enthusiasts.

ONLINE SOURCES

86 Searching for maps online
Maps are valuable tools for family and local historians alike. DAVID McVEY guides you to some of his favourite cartographic websites.

90 Using your local library
Libraries offer far more than just books these days. SIMON FOWLER looks at how family historians can use their online services.

REVIEWS

94 The most useful books
97 The latest CDs

FIRST STEPS...

There's never been a better time to start researching your family history.
Margaret Ward shows you where and how to begin

Genealogy is a hobby that can become a passion, bringing the past to life and helping you understand how your ancestors played a part in making us what we are today. With additional sources becoming available all the time, it's now even easier to trace your roots.

To make the most of these opportunities, there are a few simple tried and tested guidelines which will set you on the right path from the beginning.

While there are many advantages in having easy access to the internet, it is still possible to do research the "old fashioned way" if you don't have a computer. Libraries and record offices welcome visitors, and make a special effort to help complete beginners. Most also have computers which you can use, and may subscribe to online genealogy databases.

Old photograph albums can be an invaluable source, especially if there are captions identifying places and people. Family memorabilia also make good talking points with relatives, stirring memories and revealing interesting stories.

Remember that the best source you have when you begin is yourself. Always work back from what you know into the unknown. Start by creating a list of all the ancestors you already know about (including yourself): full names; dates of birth, marriage and, if appropriate, death (and where they are buried); where they lived; what sort of work they did; names of brothers and sisters. Put down any little detail you have, since you never know when it will become relevant.

Do tell your family what you are doing. Apart from the fact that most relatives will be interested and keen to help, you may even find that great-uncle Fred "did" the family tree 50 years ago, and that a copy has lain untouched in his daughter's attic ever since. Don't forget to keep everyone up to date with what you find out – you'll enjoy sharing your discoveries, and talking about them may jog more memories.

Before you talk to elderly relations, draw up a list of questions you want to ask. However, if someone drops a hint about a different aspect of the family, be prepared to drop the script for a while and pursue what could be an interesting trail.

Collect any relevant documents; not just birth, marriage or death certificates, but also letters and diaries. You should also hunt down medals, heirlooms and other bits and pieces of family memorabilia which may have lain untouched in a drawer for years. Photographs are particularly good talking points; sharing them is sure to bring out a few long-forgotten names and stories.

Try putting your surname into an internet search engine such as Google, a website like www.genesreunited.co.uk. Alternatively, joining a genealogy or county mailing list, could link you to other family historians around the world with the same interests (or even to long-lost relatives).

On the subject of surnames, remember that your name has probably been spelled in many different ways over the centuries. Our ancestors had no notion about "correct" spelling, while officials might write down a further different version.

Joining a group of like-minded people can give you

TINA-PRO COPY 1/481

fresh impetus. Every county has at least one family history society which will be delighted to welcome you as a member. Not only do you meet people with similar interests (and similar problems), but you can register your surname as a "member's interest". To find a society in your area, ask at a local library or record office, or visit www.ffhs.org.uk. There's more about family history societies on page 84.

If you are not sure which line of your family to pursue,

Living memories are more potent than any official document. The Fleckney family, pictured here in 1905, had five generations alive at the same time. This was most unusual for the period when most people died earlier than they do today.

Handy Hints

Be methodical

■ Always note carefully where you found information. You may want to look it up again, or confirm why you made a particular decision.

■ Organise your material. You will soon be swamped by paper, and material is easily lost.

■ If you want to use a computer program to store and organise your family history, find one that's right for you by reading reviews in family history magazines, or talking to fellow researchers. A great free one is www.geni.org.

■ Always back up your records, on computer or on paper. Keep a master copy somewhere safe.

■ Concentrate on one branch of the family, or an individual. It's easier to research an unusual name.

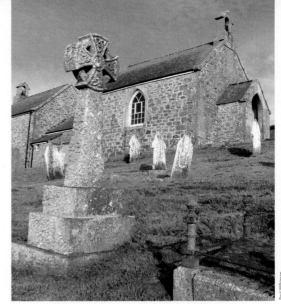

Gravestones can reveal interesting facts about a family.

choose the branch which has an unusual surname because it is usually easier to research.

You'll find help in tracking down government records and other sources at **www.familyrecords.gov.uk** where topics include wills, military records, emigration, immigration and the certificates of births, marriages and deaths kept by the General Register Office (GRO). The GRO records are essential for taking your family tree back to the early 1800s. See our article on page 12 on how to use these certificates.

The second most important official source is census returns, which let you "see" a family – hopefully all at home together – on one particular night. A census has been taken every decade since 1801 (except in 1941), although only since 1841 have the national returns listed everybody. On page 16 we explain where to find census returns, and how to use them.

Discovering a place of birth on the census could lead you to parish records and back into the 18th century. Read our article on page 64 about using these records.

Genealogy would never have captured our imagination if it were simply a matter of names and dates; there are many other ways of tracing our ancestors' footsteps.

Once you have an address, or know the area where they lived, look it up on a map. If a visit is feasible, you can walk the same streets or lanes that they trod; and take your camera, so you can create a permanent record of what you discover.

Visit the parish churchyard or local cemetery to see whether you can find family graves. In many cases memorial inscriptions have been recorded by local family history societies, which will make the search easier (see the article on page 72).

Don't forget that local museums often have displays or archives that could fill in the background on occupations and local industries, as well as day-to-day life in a previous era. Staff will usually do all they can to help.

When it comes to jobs, very few families are without a soldier or sailor among their ancestors. Finding a medal or picture of a man or woman in uniform can set you off on a whole new trail. There's a whole section about the First World War on page 50, while on page BB we explain how to track a forebear who served in the armed services.

Creating a family history is a fascinating trip into the past. Soon you will be ready to investigate national and local archives, documents such as parish registers, wills, poor law records and much more, to take your family tree back through the centuries.

There will be problems and puzzles along the way, but also many successes and excitements. Have fun!

Handy Hints

Confidentiality, consideration and copyright

■ Sometimes family historians forget – or do not realise – that they have responsibilities with regard to information they discover.

■ Respect the sensibilities of family members who may not want something they consider shameful or embarrassing to be known to all and sundry, even though it may be fascinating to you.

■ Never make public (on a website or in any other form of publication) information about living people without their permission. Be particularly careful about names, addresses, dates of birth and other details which can be used by criminals to steal identities.

■ Don't pass off other people's work as your own, even innocently. Always acknowledge your sources and always request written permission to use them when necessary.

■ Even family photographs and documents less than 70 years old may be under some form of copyright. You could need permission to reproduce them in a book or on a website.

Census returns are an important source when researching your family history.

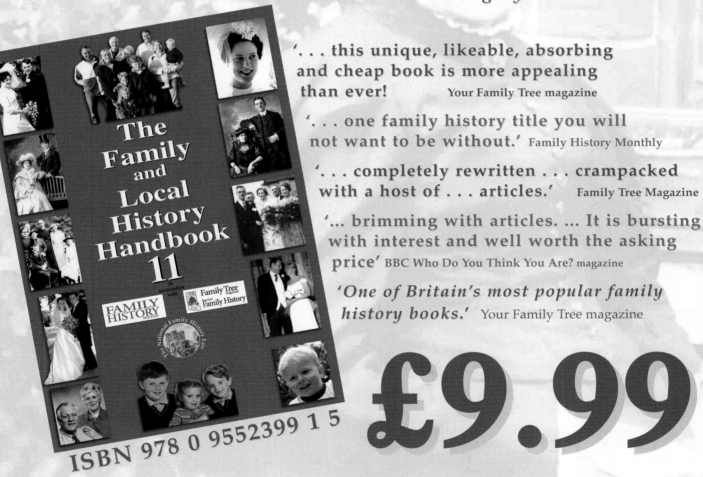

Look up your lineage
ONLINE

Many resources needed by beginners are just the click of a mouse away. **Peter Christian** guides you to the most useful family history websites

Even if all your aged relatives have email addresses, you still need to start your family history by talking to them face to face, collecting memories and other material. In addition, the first records you need – birth, marriage and death certificates – are not online. Yet there are huge resources now available on the web which can help you, with more being added on a daily basis.

There are two important points you need to know when you first start tracing your family tree: how to approach genealogical research, and which specific records you should consult. Happily, you will find plenty of answers online to both these questions.

Back to basics

Probably the most concise introduction to family history on the web is Roy Stockdill's *"Newbies" Guide to Genealogy and Family History* on Genuki at **www.genuki.org.uk/gs**

For more detailed guidance, The National Archives (TNA) website has extensive introductory material at **www.nationalarchives.gov.uk/pathways/ familyhistory** which covers all the main topics, including migration and military records.

Another good site is the BBC's Family History section at **www.bbc.co.uk/ history/familyhistory** This site includes

material relating to the *Who Do You Think You Are?* TV series, while a Family History Trail provides a step-by-step guide to what is involved in researching your ancestors.

Genealogy.com's Learning Center has guides on all aspects of genealogical research at **www.genealogy.com/genehelp.html**, with a "Getting Started" section at **www.genealogy.com/getting_started.html**. Much of the advice is specific to American records, but the general material on how to approach family history is relevant.

Both the Society of Genealogists (SoG) and the Federation of Family History Societies have a range of beginners' leaflets online, at **www.sog.org.uk/leaflets/leaflets.shtml** and **www.ffhs.org.uk/tips/first.php**, respectively.

Another introduction to genealogical records is provided by FamilyRecords at **www.familyrecords.gov.uk** which is the official government gateway to genealogical information for the UK.

Family history societies have some equally useful advice pages. Buckinghamshire Family History Society for example, provides a Family History Wiki **www.bucksfhs.org.uk/ index.php?option=com_mambowiki&Itemi d=90**, with information on a range of subjects, such as "Dates and the Calendar" and "Parish Registers". Meanwhile Berkshire Family History Society (**www.berksfhs.org.uk/ miscellaneous/startingFamilyHistory.htm**), and Somerset & Dorset Family History Society (**www.sdfhs.org/getting_started.htm**) are among those which offer more conventional beginner's guides on their websites.

Pay-per-view sites

You'll soon realise that you will have to pay to download most of the genealogical data now available online. You may grumble but a year's subscription could well be cheaper than

travelling to The National Archives once or twice a year.

You'll either need to buy a certain number of units or a subscription for a specific period. Full details are given on each site. Look out for free trials or special offers. Some libraries also provide free access to the databases provided by these sites.

www.ancestry.co.uk has many more resources than the others, including all English and Welsh censuses between 1841 and 1901, surviving First World War Army service records, historic telephone directories, and indexes to BMD records.

www.findmypast.com provides indexes to BMD records, most of the censuses, and passenger lists from Britain to ports outside Europe between 1890 and 1960.

www.familyrelatives.com contains indexes to BMD and some related material. There are some nice touches such as a tool which calculates the average age when your ancestors died.

www.thegenealogist.co.uk offers indexes to BMD certificates, censuses, and pre-1837 Nonconformist parish registers.

www.nationalarchives.gov.uk/ documentsonline allows you to download a wide range of images from The National Archives holdings for £3.50 each.

Finding help

While the guides suggested above give basic advice, they won't supply answers to specific questions which may arise during your research. The good news is that as well as providing information and data, the internet can also be an excellent source of help in solving problems.

The best places to turn to are mailing lists and message boards devoted to genealogy. Genuki's Mailing Lists page at **www.genuki.org.uk/wg** provides links to all genealogical lists relevant to UK and Irish family history, the majority of which are hosted by RootsWeb.

The most coherent genealogical message boards covering British interests are at British-Genealogy, which has forums devoted to individual counties and places, as well as many individual topics (**www.british-genealogy. com/forums**).

Both RootsWeb and British-Genealogy allow you to search past messages. You will certainly find answers to most general questions in the archive of the GENBRIT mailing list at **http://lists.rootsweb.com/index/other/ Newsgroup_Gateways/GENBRIT.html**.

If you are looking for very specific advice, it

Search engines

Don't forget to enter your ancestors' name into a search engine. You may be surprised by what you come up with. Google, of course, is the largest, but there are others which may be worth trying as they tend to come up with slightly different results. You should use a modifier like putting the name into speech marks: "John Smith" will come up with all John Smiths, rather than all Johns and all Smiths. And you may need to include other search terms like a place or occupation, such as "John Smith" Kent or "John Smith" farmer to narrow the search down further.

www.google.co.uk

will be worth searching for a discussion forum devoted to that area.

For example, the various mailing lists devoted to occupations, such as coalminers or the police, will have much more collective expertise on these occupations and their records than more general lists, while county lists and forums will be the best places for local queries.

Organising information

Once your work is under way, you need to plan your research and document what you've done.

The SoG has a very concise guide, *Note taking and keeping for genealogists*, at **www.sog.org.uk/leaflets**, and there is also useful material in Genealogy.com's "Getting Organized" pages at **www.genealogy.com/ getting_organized.html**, with detailed help on how to document your sources.

An essential beginner's tool is a genealogy database to store information on individual ancestors. Several databases can be downloaded free of charge to start you off, even if you decide to go for something more sophisticated later. Have a look at Personal Ancestral File on the FamilySearch site at **www.familysearch.org** – it's under "Order/Download Products" – or Legacy, downloadable from **www.legacyfamilytree.com**.

Alternatively you can place your family tree online. There are many sites which allow you to do this, although you should always be careful about what personal information you add about people who are still alive or died within the last five to ten years. The largest site is **www.genesreunited.com**, but if you just want to make your research available to relatives – and nobody else – then **www.geni.com** is a good choice.

There are, of course, many more sites that you will find useful. Finally, if you're just starting to trace your family tree, buy a good book on the subject – and you can do this online, too!

Cyndi's List

Nearly 300,000 links to genealogical websites can be found at **www.cyndislist.com**. They are simply arranged by category – there are 12,500 links to websites on England alone.

CERTIFICATES

Birth, marriage and death certificates are some of the most important records you will use in your research. They date back to July 1837

BIRTH CERTIFICATES

These are a core resource for family historians. Admittedly buying a copy is expensive – £7 each at time of writing – but they can be very informative. Although registration of births was not made compulsory until 1874, it is clear that even before then, almost all parents registered their children. If you can't find a birth, it is likely that there is a problem with the indexes or that the name by which you know an ancestor is not the one he or she was given at birth, rather than that it was not registered.

The value of these certificates is not simply confined to the life event they record; they give you more clues to follow up. A birth certificate names the father and mother (including her maiden name), their address, and the father's occupation. Armed with this information, you can look for the parents' marriage certificate.

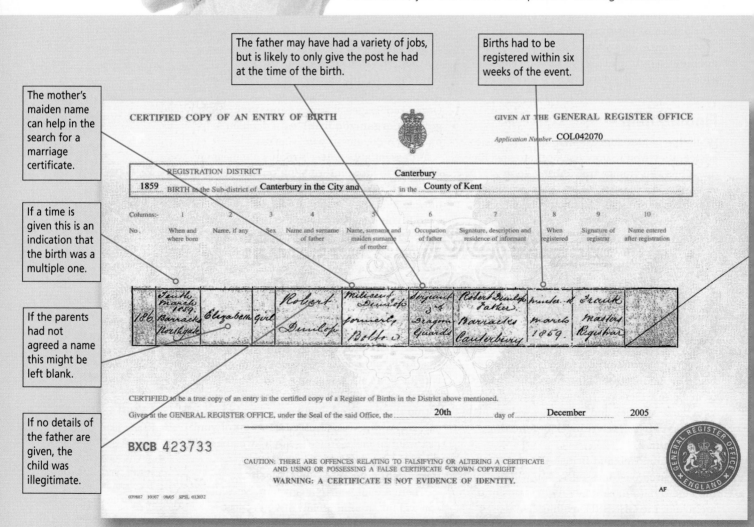

The father may have had a variety of jobs, but is likely to only give the post he had at the time of the birth.

Births had to be registered within six weeks of the event.

The mother's maiden name can help in the search for a marriage certificate.

If a time is given this is an indication that the birth was a multiple one.

If the parents had not agreed a name this might be left blank.

If no details of the father are given, the child was illegitimate.

CERTIFIED COPY OF AN ENTRY OF BIRTH

GIVEN AT THE GENERAL REGISTER OFFICE

Application Number COL042070

REGISTRATION DISTRICT — Canterbury

1859 BIRTH in the Sub-district of Canterbury in the City and — in the County of Kent

Columns:-	1	2	3	4	5	6	7	8	9	10
No.	When and where born	Name, if any	Sex	Name and surname of father	Name, surname and maiden surname of mother	Occupation of father	Signature, description and residence of informant	When registered	Signature of registrar	Name entered after registration

CERTIFIED to be a true copy of an entry in the certified copy of a Register of Births in the District above mentioned.

Given at the GENERAL REGISTER OFFICE, under the Seal of the said Office, the ____ 20th ____ day of ____ December ____ 2005

BXCB 423733

CAUTION: THERE ARE OFFENCES RELATING TO FALSIFYING OR ALTERING A CERTIFICATE AND USING OR POSSESSING A FALSE CERTIFICATE ©CROWN COPYRIGHT
WARNING: A CERTIFICATE IS NOT EVIDENCE OF IDENTITY.

MARRIAGE CERTIFICATES

After official registration began, for the first time couples could choose a civil ceremony, although few initially did so. Couples who married in a church, chapel or synagogue would automatically be registered as part of the ceremony.

If you don't already have a date for a marriage, start looking around the date of the first known child's birth, then continue to search the indexes backwards in time, remembering that they could have married 20 or so years before then. If that fails, look forward from the birth date. Of course, it is possible the couple never married. Until the 1920s divorce was very difficult for ordinary people and many couples decided to separate without going through legal proceedings. They could not remarry, but anyone with a new partner could easily hide this fact to avoid gossip or local scandal.

Often if both bride and bridegroom were over the age of 21 this would be noted as "of full age". It is not unusual for ages to be changed either to make an individual appear older (particularly if they were under 21) or younger (perhaps to minimise a large disparity in ages between the spouses).

If a marriage took place in a church, an identical entry should have been made in the parish register or its equivalent.

If the same address is given this is not generally because they were cohabiting. Either they gave the bride's address (occasionally the bridegroom's) so they could marry at her church, or they were "living" at an address for 21 days before the wedding so they could marry in the church of their choice.

Often ignored by researchers, the witnesses were normally family members or friends, which could give further clues to relationships. The cross by Lydia Small's name indicates that she made her mark rather than signed the register.

DEATH CERTIFICATES

Often simply seen as the full stop at the end of a life, death certificates can provide plenty of useful information worth following up. Look for instance, at who registered the death, and their relationship to the deceased.

Handy Hints

Ordering certificates

Today we are still using much the same system for registering births, marriages and deaths that began on 1 July 1837 in England and Wales.

Events are registered in the local register office (or church for marriages). From here, superintendent registrars send copies of entries in the registers to the General Register Office (GRO) in London once a quarter (March, June, September and December). From this, the national index can be compiled.

These indexes are widely available on microfiche at The National Archives, local record offices and some major libraries. However, most people now search them online. The best place to start is **www.freebmd.org.uk** which, as the name suggests, is free, although it is not yet complete. There are also several commercial sites offering GRO indexes, including **www.genesreunited.com**, **www.ancestry.co.uk** and **www.findmypast.com**.

Once you have found the entry you want and noted down the reference number, you can order a copy of the certificate either online, by phone, or by post. Each certificate costs £7 (more if you haven't noted the reference number). Order at **www.gro.gov.uk/gro/content/order_certificates/index.asp#0**, ring 0845 603 7788, or write to GRO PO Box 2, Southport PR8 2JD.

Paul Wilkinson

If the individual died in a workhouse or hospital there may be further records worth tracking down.	For accidents, murders and other unusual cause of deaths there would have been a coroner's inquest. Most coroners' records are not available, but you should be able to find a full account of the inquest in the local newspaper.	If the informant was present at the time of death then this would be recorded.

IA 853777   (Printed by authority of the Regi

CERTIFIED COPY of an 🛡 **ENTRY OF DEATH**
Pursuant to the Births and **Deaths Registration Act, 1953**

...utory fee for this certificate is 3s. 9d.
... search is necessary to find the entry,
... fee is payable in addition.

Registration District

63... **Death in the Sub-district of** ____ in the ____

When and where died	Name and surname	Sex	Age	Occupation	Cause of death	Signature, description, and residence of informant	When registered	Signature of registrar
1	2	3	4	5	6	7	8	9
Twenty Eighth November 1963. 6. Manor Close Henfield	Gertrude Louise Chater.	Female	45 years	Wife of Frank Chater a Fitter (Retired)	1a Bronchopneumonia b. Bilateral hemiplegia c. Carotid insufficiency and generalised Arteriosclerosis II Diabetes mellitus certified by Paul Wellings MB	G.K. Chater Son Y. Morrison House High Street Feltham	Twenty ninth November 1963.	J R Mayes. Registrar

...eph Reginald Mayes, Registrar of Births and Deaths for the Sub-district of ____ , in the COUNTY OF ____
do hereby certify that this is a true copy of Entry No. 54 in the Register Book of Deaths for the said Sub-district, and that such Register
...s now legally in my custody.

WITNESS MY HAND this 29TH day of November, 1963.

J R Mayes.
Registrar of Births and Deaths.

...N.—Any person who (1) falsifies any of the particulars on this certificate,
... uses a falsified certificate as true, knowing it to be false, is liable to
...cution.

Making sense of the CENSUS

Every 10 years the government takes a census which should tell us who lived where on that particular evening. **Simon Fowler** enumerates what you might find in these vital records

Census records are some of the most important – and most interesting – records you will use in researching your ancestors. They offer a fascinating snapshot of your family, their relationships to each other, their address and the way they lived on a specific night.

You can even find out who their neighbours were, and what they all did for a living. Census indexes may also allow you to find family members who were away from home that evening.

With the exception of 1941, a census has been taken every 10 years since 1801. The first census act was passed by Parliament in November 1800, and the count was taken three months later – an incredibly short period of time. Local officials found that nine million people lived in England and Wales, although we do not know who they were as few names or other individual details were collected.

By the late 1830s the Royal Statistical Society and others were pressing for more detailed questions, although there was considerable opposition from people who feared an infringement of their civil liberties. The first census to contain details of every individual in Great Britain was taken in 1841, but even this is less informative than later ones. More detailed questions were asked in 1851 and subsequent censuses.

Officials, known as enumerators, distributed questionnaires a few days before census night to heads of household (normally the senior male). The enumerators returned a few days later to collect the completed paperwork and help people who were illiterate to fill in the forms. Once all the questionnaires had been collected, the information was entered into books, which were then sent to Whitehall for processing. With a very few exceptions, the original forms have been destroyed, so it is these census enumerators' books which survive.

Census records for 1841, 1851, 1861, 1871, 1881, 1891 and 1901 are available. Those for 1911 will become available in early 2009.

What you can find in the records

The answers people gave to the questions are not only very informative, but can lead you to other records about particular individuals, or

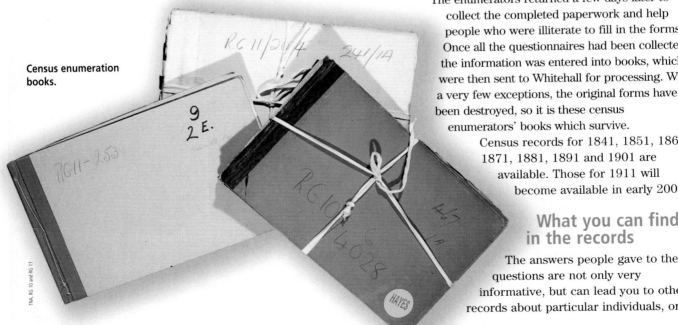

Census enumeration books.

TNA, RG 10 and RG 11

help take your search back in time. You can discover:

■ Full names, sex, marital status, age, and where people were living on census night – even if this was not their usual address. Anyone travelling overnight by train or at sea was registered at the place they arrived the next morning. In 1841, however, one enthusiastic enumerator managed to record everybody on the overnight train between London and Southampton!

■ Their relationship to the head of the household – who was usually the oldest man.

■ Their occupation, although this could be misleading at times. Very few prostitutes are included, although there were tens of thousands of women engaged in "the oldest profession".

■ Their birthplace. In 1841 this was noted as either in the county or outside, but from 1851 the parish had to be included as well. For anyone born in Scotland, Ireland or abroad it was sufficient just to put the country of birth, and whether they were blind, deaf, dumb or insane.

FILLING UP THE CENSUS PAPER.

Wife of his Bosom. "Upon my word, Mr. Peewitt! Is this the Way you Fill up your Census? So you call Yourself the 'Head of the Family'—do you—and me a 'Female?'"

Cartoon from *Punch*, 1851.

■ In addition, from 1891 people had to indicate whether they were employed, self-employed, or unemployed. This question was often misunderstood, so the answers are unreliable. In Wales, they were asked whether they could speak Welsh, Welsh and English, or just English. Similar questions were asked in the Isle of Man, Scotland and Ireland.

■ In 1911 married women were required to state the number of years they had been married, and the number of their children born alive and the number still living. In that census more information was also required about an individual's occupation and nationality.

Where to find them

Census records from 1841 onwards have been fully transcribed and digitised and can be seen online at various commercial sites. In general, using the name indexes is free, while you pay to view a transcript (where this is provided) or the original census return itself. The quality of the indexing varies, so you may need to use a lot of imagination to find your ancestor. In one index for the 1881 census, for example, the great German philosopher Karl Marx is indexed as Karl Wass.

There is a full (and free) surname index for the British 1881 census, which gives you almost all the information you would find on the original documents, at **www.familysearch.org**.

The following websites provide paid-for access to all or part of the censuses. Charges

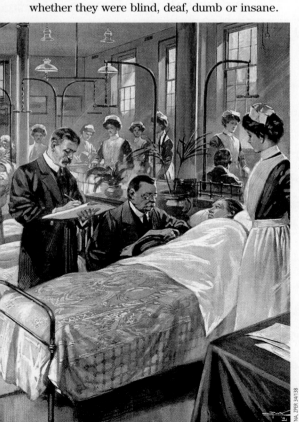

An enumerator performs the difficult task of obtaining information from a hospital patient for the 1911 census.

Coming soon...

The 1911 census will be released in 2009. Read more about it in *Ancestors*, or online at **www. 1911census.co.uk**.

vary, so shop around or take advantage of any special offers.

www.ancestry.co.uk
www.findmypast.com
www.genesreunited.com
www.thegenealogist.co.uk
www.scotlandspeople.gov.uk (Scotland only)

Almost all Irish census records before 1901 have been destroyed. Those for 1901 and 1911 are being digitised and made available, free, at **www.census.nationalarchives.ie**.

If you prefer to use copies on microfilm, The National Archives at Kew has a complete set for England and Wales, while most county archives and local studies libraries will have ones for their locality. Access to these is free.

In Scotland you will find a similar service at the Family History Centre in Edinburgh.

For Irish census records visit The National Archives in Dublin (all Ireland), and the Public Record Office of Northern Ireland (six counties).

How to read the census

This is an example of a page from an 1881 census enumerator's book for the St Pancras district of London. The other censuses, with the exception of 1841, look much the same and contain similar information.

Potential pitfalls and problems

■ Entries may appear to be scored out – this was done in London by the clerks who were analysing the returns – which can make them difficult to read.
■ About 5–10 per cent of the 1861 census is missing, as is a small part of 1851.

Sometimes there's no address in small villages. In towns, the street numbering may well have changed since the census was taken so it may not be possible to find the exact house an ancestor lived in.

A double line usually means a new house, and a single line means two or more households (or families) in a single house.

Indexers may get the names wrong – so if you are using online indexes in particular, you may need to use a lot of lateral thinking to find an individual.

The head of the household or family was normally the oldest man.

Local government or ecclesiastical unit where the census conducted.

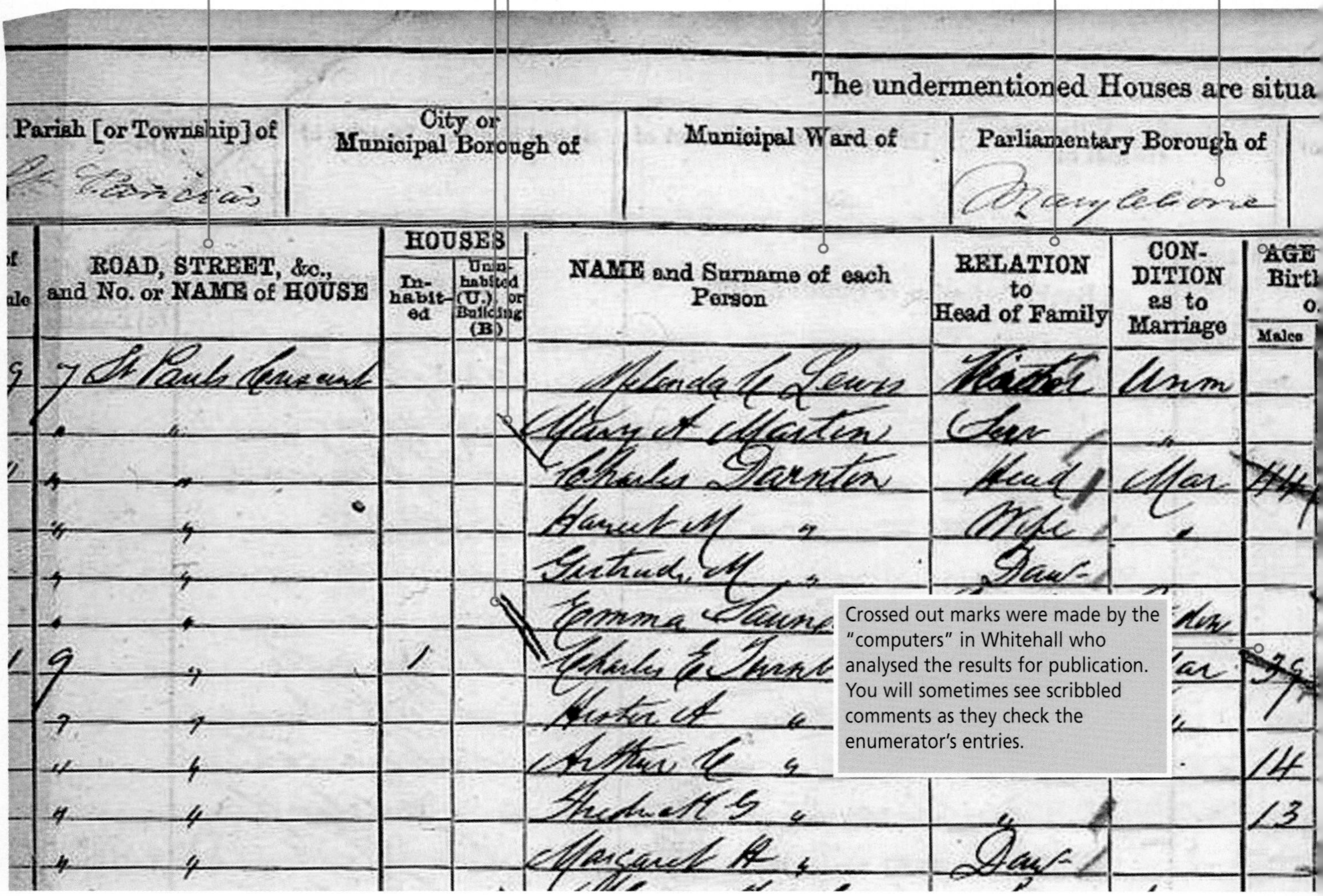

Crossed out marks were made by the "computers" in Whitehall who analysed the results for publication. You will sometimes see scribbled comments as they check the enumerator's entries.

Perhaps five per cent of the population do not appear in the census, either because they were sleeping rough, not at home, or the enumerator forgot to include them.

The age given by individuals is often a year or two out – either people did not know their correct age, or they did not want the government to know it.

The occupation given can often be misleading.

It can be difficult to work out where people were born – either the details are incomplete or the parish given does not exist. This was often because the enumerator misheard what he was told.

People in Victorian times moved far more frequently than we might suppose. If they aren't where they should be on census night, the chances are that they remained near their old address. It is worth checking to see whether they are still in the district, or perhaps staying with relatives.

What the census can also tell you

As well as telling you about your direct ancestors, census records can provide other information, such as: relations, lodgers and servants in the household.

If relatives of the wife are resident (this is normally made clear in the relationship to the householder column) you may discover the wife's maiden name, and perhaps something about her family as well.

You can sometimes track the movement of a family around the country by the birthplaces given for the children.

Using information in the birthplace column for adults, you can check parish registers for their christening.

Ages often vary a year or two between censuses. In 1841 the ages of children under 14 were given in full, for adults they were rounded down to the nearest five years, although many enumerators gave the full age.

Usually self-evident. Although children were often recorded as scholars, this did not necessarily mean they attended school. Employers were supposed to give the number of people they employed and farmers the number of acres farmed.

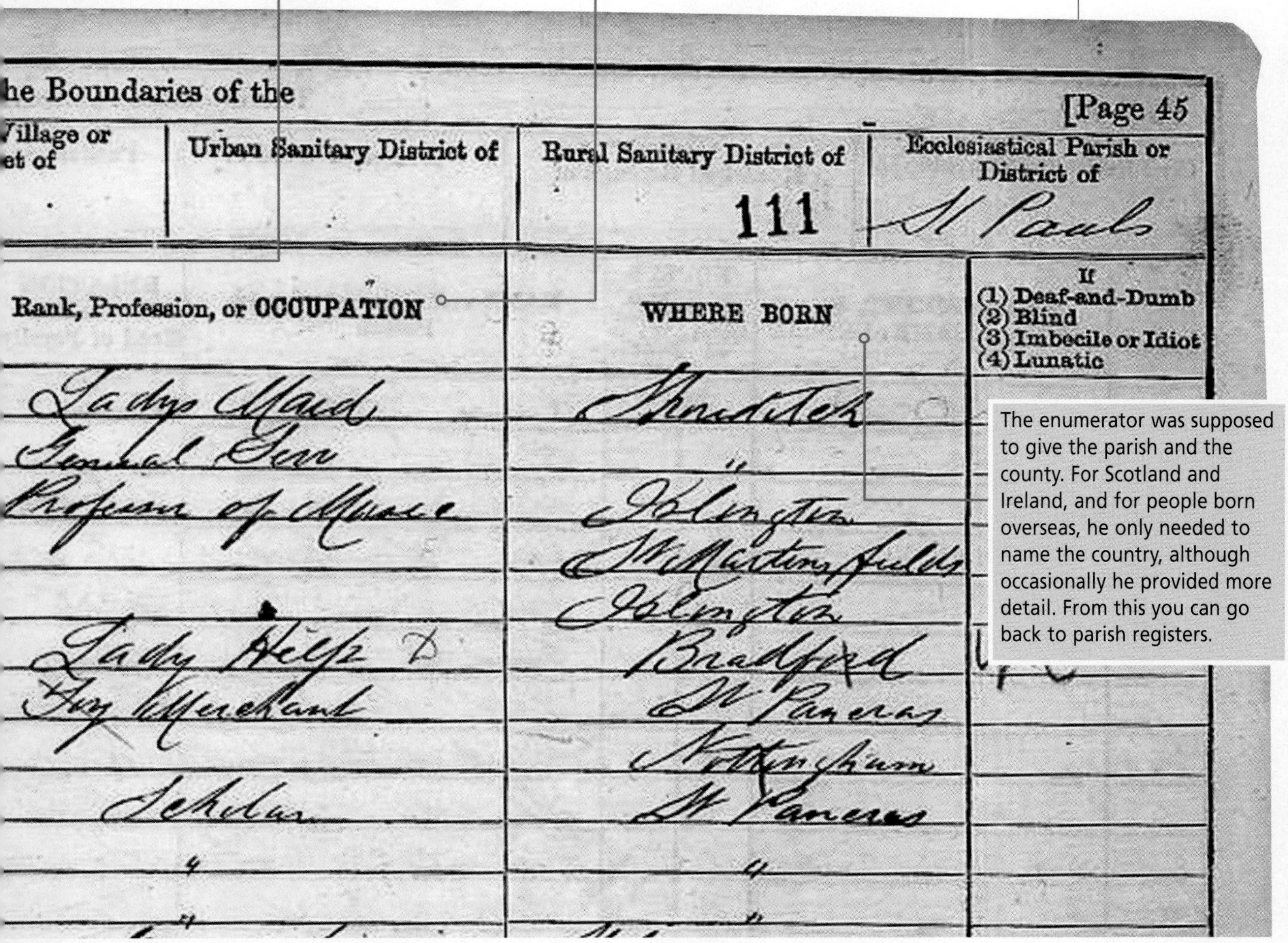

The enumerator was supposed to give the parish and the county. For Scotland and Ireland, and for people born overseas, he only needed to name the country, although occasionally he provided more detail. From this you can go back to parish registers.

---

he Boundaries of the

[Page 45]

Village or ...et of	Urban Sanitary District of	Rural Sanitary District of	Ecclesiastical Parish or District of
		111	St Pauls

Rank, Profession, or OCCUPATION	WHERE BORN	If (1) Deaf-and-Dumb (2) Blind (3) Imbecile or Idiot (4) Lunatic
Ladys Maid	Shoreditch	
General Serv	"	
Professor of Music	Islington	
	St Martins fields	
	Islington	
Lady Help	Bradford	
Fsr Merchant	St Pancras	
	Nottingham	
Scholar	St Pancras	

Benefit from a

Whether your ancestors owned large swathes of land or came from a more humble background, the chances are that some of them have left behind wills, outlining what they wanted to happen to their possessions after death. **David Annal** explains what you can gain from reading a last testament

Wills are a truly remarkable source for family historians: not only do they contain invaluable information about family relationships, but the fact that they were written by our ancestors themselves gives them the sort of authority and authenticity that documents created by the government or the Church so often lack.

A couple of crucial points to consider before you start a search for a will. First of all you should be aware that prior to the passing of the Married Women's Property Act in 1881 you will not, as a rule, find wills for married women, only for widows and spinsters. It's also important to remember that until fairly recent times the vast majority of the population, men or women, simply didn't leave a will. That's not to say that you shouldn't look for one, just that you shouldn't be too surprised if you don't find anything.

On 12 January 1858, a new civic system of proving wills (that is, the process by which a will was accepted as a legally valid document) was introduced – basically the one still in use today. Since medieval times, the responsibility of proving wills had been in the hands of the Church of England through a vast network of ecclesiastical courts. But from 1858 the state took over, and district probate registries were set up around the country to handle the process.

So, whenever you're planning a search for an ancestor's will, the first question to ask yourself is whether the person died before or after 1858.

Wills since 1858

Searching for a will that was proved on or after January 1858 is a relatively straightforward process. Annual indexes (known as calendars) to all wills proved in England and Wales were produced right from the start of the civil probate system. Your biggest problem here may be finding copies of the calendars, as they are not yet available on the internet, and paper and microfiche copies are rare.

A full set of calendars is held by the Principal Registry of the Family Division in its reading rooms. Some district registries also have copies, although many have given their sets to their local county record office. A small number of sets of microfiche covering the years 1858 to 1943 have also been produced, and a set is available at The National Archives in Kew. The Society of Genealogists also has a set of microfilm copies of the calendars from 1858 to 1930.

A typical entry in the calendar will tell you:
- the date of probate
- the deceased's full name
- their occupation
- when they died
- where they died
- where they lived
- where the will was proved
- the names, residences, occupations and relationships of two or more executors
- the value of the deceased's estate

In 1892 the format of the calendars changed, and from this date there is significantly less detail in each entry.

Wills before 1858

Before 1858, the situation is much more complicated. There were more than a hundred church courts where wills could be proved; there is no centralised index; and surviving records of the courts are now spread around the country in local and county record offices.

A 19th century portrait of William Shakespeare, copied from an illustration in Venetian State Papers. Below, part of his will which he wrote in March 1616. He died three months later of a fever. He left the bulk of his estate to his elder daughter, Susanna, while to his wife, Anne, he left "my second best bed".

I Jane Austen of the Parish of Chawton do by this my last Will & Testament give and bequeath to my dearest Sister Cassandra Eliz: every thing of which I may die possessed, or which may be hereafter due to me, subject to the payment of my Funeral Expences, & to a Legacy of £50. to my Brother Henry, & £50. to M.de Bigeon — which I request may be paid as soon as convenient. And I appoint my said dear Sister the Executrix of this my last Will & Testament.

Jane Austen

April 27. 1817

TNA, PROB 1/78

BRIDGEMAN ART LIBRARY

JANE AUSTEN'S WILL

The wills of famous people – Jane Austen's among them – are available for free from Documents Online at The National Archives.

Jane's original will was written in her own hand and since it was unwitnessed, a sworn affidavit was necessary to certify the document's authenticity.

In this instance, the affidavit was provided by John Grove Palmer and Harriet Ebel Palmer – in-laws of Charles-John Austen, Jane's brother. Cassandra Elizabeth Austen, Jane's sister, was the executrix and heiress. She was also responsible for the preservation and subsequent distribution to her brothers, nephews and nieces of Jane Austen's letters, manuscripts and memorabilia.

The system was based on the hierarchy of ancient English ecclesiastical jurisdictions, with the provinces of Canterbury and York at the top of the tree, a number of dioceses underneath (each comprising various archdeaconries and deaneries), and the smaller "peculiar" courts at the bottom. In practical terms this means that wherever your ancestors lived, their wills could have been proved in one of three or four different courts, and you will have to search the records of each of these in order to establish whether they left a will or not.

Surviving records are likely to include:
- original wills submitted to the court
- a series of registered copies entered into ledgers by the court's clerks
- a set of contemporary manuscript indexes

Over the years, a number of record offices and local and family history societies have compiled and published various will indexes, and some record offices have produced card indexes to their own holdings. But by far the most significant change in more recent years has been the advent of online probate indexes, in some cases allowing access to digital images of the wills themselves.

The most important of these online resources (and by far the largest) is the National Archives's Documents Online website at **www.nationalarchives.gov.uk/ documentsonline**.

The website provides full access to the entire collection of wills proved in the Prerogative Court of Canterbury – known more conveniently to family historians as the PCC. This was the senior court of probate for England and Wales, covering the whole of the province of Canterbury – basically England south of the River Trent and most of Wales.

The PCC also had responsibility for the wills of English and Welsh citizens who died overseas or in other parts of the United Kingdom. The collection of over one million wills dating from 1383 to 1858 includes some of the most famous names in English history: William Shakespeare, Jane Austen, Sir Isaac Newton, Lord Nelson, William Wordsworth, to name but a few.

And while it's certainly true that the majority of the wills proved in the PCC relate to people from the upper echelons of society – the nobility and gentry, military officers, merchants, lawyers, clergyman and large landowners – the records also include the wills of many small farmers, artisans, tradesmen, soldiers and sailors, and even a few agricultural labourers.

The Prerogative Court of York (the PCY) fulfilled a similar role for England's Northern counties. Its records are held by the Borthwick Institute at York University.

As you move down the hierarchy of ecclesiastical probate courts you'll find increasingly large numbers of wills of "ordinary" people.

Interpreting wills

There is simply no limit to the amount of useful detail you could find in a will. At the very least you are likely to get the testator's occupation and place of residence as well as the names of his wife and children, but you may also discover previously unknown nephews and nieces, uncles, aunts and

WILLS BEFORE 1858 DISSECTED

They usually started with the words "In the name of God Amen", reflecting both the ecclesiastical background to the process of proving wills and the highly religious nature of the society in which our ancestors lived.

• The testator's name, occupation and residence, followed by the date of the will and a statement that the testator was either "in good and perfect health, mind and memory" or possibly "sick in body but whole in mind" – the important point here was that he was fully rational and compos mentis at the time the will was written.

• The testator often left detailed instructions regarding his burial before getting on to the real business of the will – making sure that his nearest and dearest got their just deserts.

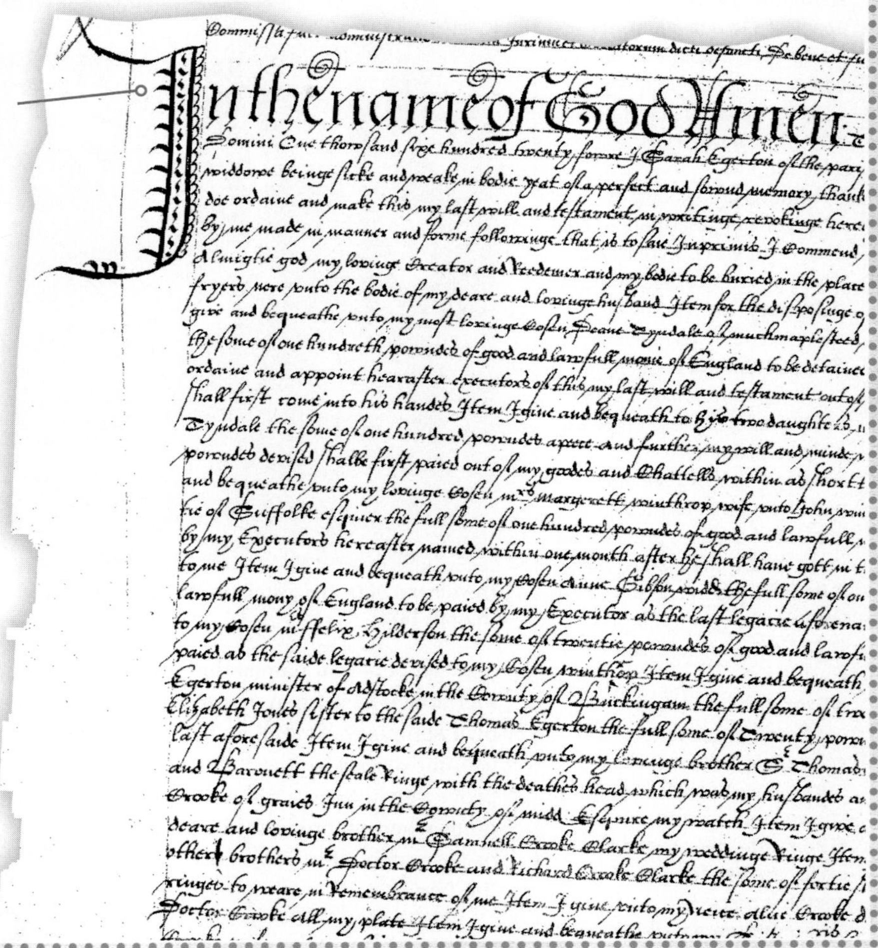

cousins, and it's not uncommon for more distant relatives to be mentioned. You may also come across references to earlier generations if, for example, the testator refers to an item which was bequeathed to him by a parent or even a grandparent.

Wills can also give you a fascinating insight into your ancestors' lives, often listing personal possessions or tools connected with their trade. Just occasionally, you might come across evidence of a family quarrel where, for example, the eldest son was "cut off with a shilling" or one of the children was left out of the will altogether, but you need to be careful about how you interpret the size of the bequests. The fact that one child was left significantly less than the others may be because they had already received a sum of money in their father's lifetime.

There are a number of problems that may confront you when you first come to read a will: there's the lack of regular punctuation; the use of archaic terms, and the occasional Latin word here or there; but it's probably

the unfamiliar handwriting that will cause you the greatest difficulty. The best advice is to get a photocopy of the will and take it home to read at your leisure. Don't try to work out every word first time through – if you get stuck on a particular word, carry on and come back to it later. The more you read old wills, the better you will get at recognising the strange characters and styles that were used by the clerks – it really is a matter of experience.

Most wills before 1858 followed a fairly standard format (as shown above). Working out exactly what the testator was trying to say can be a frustrating process – it's easy to lose track of where you are in a particular sentence as it rambles on into yet another sub-clause. And as we move into the 19th century wills start to get longer and longer, with increasingly complicated bequests and more and more detailed instructions on how the deceased's estate should be disposed of.

It's a good idea to read through the will, make notes of the various bequests, the places

Some useful terms

■ **Administrator** – A person appointed to administer the estate of an intestate or to administer in default of an executor named in a will. A woman is known as an administratrix.

■ **Admons** (also known as letters of administration) – Legal documents which were issued where an intestor died intestate.

■ **Annuity** – An income or allowance received annually.

■ **Appurtenances** – An item that belongs to something else. For example, the land on which a house is situated.

■ **Assign or assignee** – A person who is appointed to act in place of another, often found in the phrase "heirs and assigns".

■ **Beneficiary** – A person who is left something in a will.

■ **Codicil** – A supplement to a will.

■ **Executor** – A person appointed by the testator to ensure that his wishes are carried out. A female executor is known as an executrix.

■ **Heir** – The person who is legally entitled to succeed to another's property.

■ **Hereditaments** – Property that can be inherited.

■ **Imprimis** – First (Latin).

■ **Intestate** – A person who dies without leaving a will.

■ **Messuage** – A house or dwelling-place together with its appurtenances.

■ **Personal estate** – A person's moveable property not including land and buildings, etc.

■ **Probate** – Proving a will. The act of making it a legally binding document.

■ **Real estate** – The land and buildings, etc (ie not moveable property) owned by a person.

■ **Testator** – A man who makes a will. A woman is known as a testatrix.

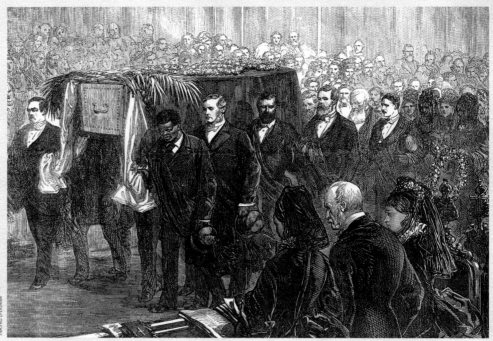

TNA PRO ZPER34464

The funeral of Dr Livingstone in Westminster Abbey, as depicted in the *Illustrated London News* of 25 April 1874.

and the personal names that are mentioned in it, then create your own summary. As well as being a useful exercise in itself, this will prove valuable as a quick reference point when planning future research or assessing what you know about the family.

Administrations and inventories

Before we leave the world of probate, there are a couple of other documents to look at that are closely associated with wills.

If a person died without leaving a will, letters of administration could be granted to their next of kin or another person who had a claim to the deceased's estate. Letters of administration (commonly known as admons) were granted by the same courts that were responsible for proving wills, with the same change in 1858 from an ecclesiastical to a civil system. In fact, the post-1858 national indexes to admons are combined with the probate calendars, which makes searching for these documents quite straightforward. Unfortunately for our purposes, the amount of information that you get on letters of administration is quite limited: usually just the name, date of death, residence and

occupation of the deceased, as well as the name of the administrator, together with their occupation, place of residence and relationship to the deceased. Occasionally, there may be some other detail which could

SPOKEN OR NUNCUPATIVE WILLS

Spoken wills usually occurred when the testator had left the drafting of a will to the last minute and was on his or her deathbed. By law, It was necessary for at least two witnesses to be present when the words were spoken, and for them to be aware that the testator was making his will. The words were written down and signed as soon as possible, normally following the death of the testator.

Following the Wills Act of 1837, nuncupative wills were declared invalid unless made by soldiers or sailors on active service.

One very strange spoken will was that of John Plate in 1718. Not only were his last wishes recorded by John Descrambes but also the manner of his death. It appears that he was "having at some time before his death been indisposed or disordered in his mind but having lucid or intelligent intervals but in one of his lunatick fits did on Thursday the tenth day of Aprill 1718 being at his lodgings in Cecill Court near St Martin's Lane stab himself into the breast with a penknife in several places which wounds he shortly after died" (PROB 11/564 f.361-362). During his lucid moments, he managed to speak his last will, which was duly proved by the court.

Right, early wills often include instructions for the disposal of the body, sometimes giving details of location for burial, sometimes with more unusual requests. The will of Weilliam Blackett (right), proved in 1782, requested that 'my body may be kept as long as it shall not be offensive and that one or more of my toes or fingers may be cut off to secure a certainty of my being dead and if I depart this mortal life at Plymouth I desire to be buried in a private cheap and decent a manner as possible'.

provide you with vital information about the family, and it's always worth checking for an admon if your search for a will was unsuccessful. However, you certainly shouldn't assume that because there isn't a will there must be an admon – this is far from being the case.

It was not uncommon before the late 1700s for an inventory to be taken, listing the deceased's personal possessions, often on a room-by-room basis, together with the value of each item and a total value of the estate. Inventories don't survive in huge numbers but those that do will give you a fascinating insight into an ancestor's daily life.

Death duty records

Both admons and inventories are usually kept with the collections of wills among the records of the old ecclesiastical courts; but there's another source, closely related to wills, for which we have to thank the Inland Revenue. A vast series of registers was kept between the years 1796 and 1903 recording the payments of a series of taxes known collectively as death duty. Copies of all wills proved in England and

How to buy post-1858 wills

Wills currently cost £5 and are available by post from the York Probate Sub Registry, First floor, Castle Chambers, 5 Clifford Street, York YO1 9RG; telephone 01904 666777; **www.hmcourts-service.gov.uk**.

Alternatively, get them in person from The Principal Probate Registry, First Avenue House, 42–49 High Holborn, London WC1V 6NP; telephone 020 7947 6939.

Wales were sent by the various probate courts to the Inland Revenue, where clerks began their work by abstracting the details of the various bequests and beneficiaries and copying the information into their registers.

These death duty registers have a particular value for family historians for a number of reasons. First of all, they identify the name of the court where the will was proved, which in the absence of a pre-1858 national probate index can save you a great deal of searching. Second, the registers were living, working documents: the Inland Revenue went to great pains to ensure that it collected every penny due, and information about payments was recorded meticulously and in great detail. If it learnt that a beneficiary had died, the date of death would be noted; if an executor moved house, the new address was entered; if a daughter married, her married name was recorded.

Sometimes a will may simply indicate that the testator had a number of children, while the equivalent entry in the death duty registers might actually name them. You could even learn about children who were born after the testator wrote his will.

There are, admittedly, a few difficulties you might encounter while using the registers. For a start, you'll need to be able to get to The National Archives in Kew to view the documents, although indexes are online at **www.findmypast.com**. Second, when you do see the registers, you'll find that they can be quite difficult to interpret, to say the least because the notes made by the Inland Revenue clerks, recording the receipt of new information concerning the case, are often written in a heavily abbreviated style which can sometimes obscure their meaning. The clerks clearly knew what they meant at the time but it's not always obvious to us today, and after several years of annotations, an entry in the registers can become quite confusing. The entries were only "closed" once the Inland Revenue was satisfied either that it had collected all the tax due, or that the estate was for one reason or another exempt from payment of duty. And since examples have been found of notes being entered in the registers more than 70 years after a file was opened, you can imagine just how congested the entries can become.

All these records can be extremely useful in your research, both for the vast amount of information they can provide and for the number of other records they can lead you into. The most obvious are records of deaths and burials, but they can also suggest links to census returns, births and baptisms, marriages and even more "advanced" sources concerning land ownership and legal disputes.

Wills are a vital resource for family historians, and although accessing and interpreting the records may present you with some difficulties, you should make every possible effort to track them down and take the time to learn what they're telling us about the lives of our ancestors.

This is an edited extract from *Easy Family History: The stress-free guide to starting your research* by David Annal, published by The National Archives at £6.99.

USEFUL SOURCES

The Prerogative Court of York records are held by the Borthwick Institute, University of York, Heslington, York YO10 5DD; telephone 01904 321166; **www.york.ac.uk/borthwick**.

The National Archives at Kew holds sets of microfiche of pre-1858 Prerogative Court of Canterbury (PCC) wills, along with a set of the National Probate Calendar between 1858 and 1943. You can buy copies of PCC wills online at **www.nationalarchives.gov.uk/documentsonline** and there is a detailed index.

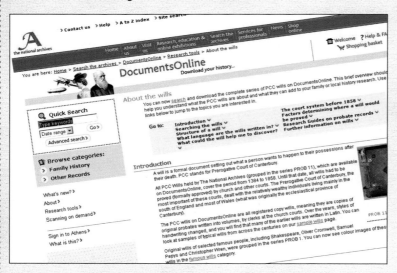

The Society of Genealogists, also has set of the National Probate Calendar and many indexes and catalogues to pre-1858 wills proven in courts other than the PCC. The SoG is a 14 Charterhouse buildings, Goswell Road, London EC1M 7BA; telephone 020 7251 8799; **www.sog.org.uk**.

The probate system in Scotland was very different to that in the rest of the British Isles. Details of testaments, as wills were known, between 1513 and 1901 are at **www.scotlandspeople.gov.uk**.

Many Irish wills before the First World War were destroyed by fire in 1922, but some information can be gleaned from surviving calendars. Details at **www.ireland.com/ancestor/browse/ records/wills/abstract.htm**.

Read more about it
Articles about wills appeared in issues 1, 23, 44 and 56 of *Ancestors* magazine. See page 93 for details about buying back issues.

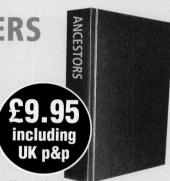

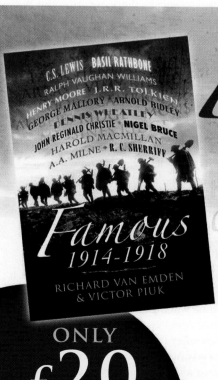

Making the best use of Kew

In the course of your family history researches, you are almost certain to use the records held by The National Archives. **Simon Fowler** offers some advice about getting the most out of your visit

Top tip

References

The National Archives's records are arranged by the government department which created them and then into series – that is, type of record. Thus pre-1913 soldiers' documents are in series WO 97 – the prefix WO standing for War Office and 97 the number which was assigned to the series. Individual items, called pieces, are given a unique number, so WO 97/1677 contains service records for men in the 100th Regiment of Foot between 1855 and 1872.

The National Archives has been caring for the nation's archival records for over 150 years. Now, some ten million individual files, books and documents are stored in well over 100 miles of shelving at its headquarters at Kew. And as well as looking after paper and parchment The National Archives is leading ambitious projects to preserve the electronic records (emails, websites and the like) which are being created today across Whitehall.

Kew has the raw material for historical researchers on every subject in which the British government had an interest in. For example, there are newly released files about Unidentified Flying Objects, case papers on infamous murders, patented designs for dresses, and combat reports from the Battle of Britain. Perhaps the most famous document is the Domesday Book, which records in great detail all the holders of land in 1086, but there are also Shakespeare's will, Cabinet minutes and even Elton John's name change.

You can use The National Archives in two ways. An increasing proportion of the most popular material – notably census records, passenger lists, pre-1858 wills and First World War service documents – is available online. This is being done in partnership with commercial companies, such as Ancestry and Findmypast, who make a small charge to access these records. But it saves you a journey to Kew, and the quality of the indexing and the images themselves is very high.

Alternatively you are welcome to visit The National Archives to check out the records for yourself. It doesn't cost anything and there are lots of helpful staff to point you in the right direction. And don't forget the half-hour orientation session at 11.30 every day showing first time visitors how to get started. There's no need to book, just turn up. There are also regular talks at 2pm; a list of forthcoming ones appears in every issue of *Ancestors*.

Before you come

There's a lot you can do before you visit Kew. It may seem tedious but it can save you a lot of precious time when you are there.

The National Archives website's pages on visiting Kew offer lots of useful advice for visitors (**www.nationalarchives.gov.uk/visit**). There's even a virtual tour if you want to see what the reading rooms are like for yourself.

Why not read up on what records are

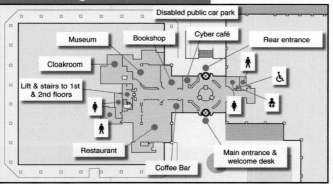

Plan of the ground floor at Kew

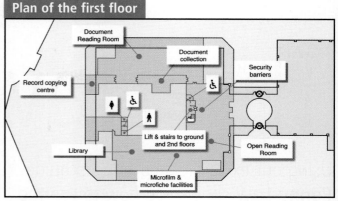

Plan of the first floor

available and what they will tell you by consulting the range of research guides. You will be able to work out which records are likely to help you on your visit and ensure you don't waste your time by looking for material which may not exist. They can be downloaded from The National Archives website at **www.nationalarchives.gov.uk/ gettingstarted**.

Using the online catalogue (**www.nationalarchives.gov.uk/catalogue**) will give you the references for any records you need to see when you visit. It is similar in structure to search engines, such as Google, and there are help pages available if you get confused.

Lastly, you can order documents which will be ready when you arrive – this can save precious time if you have come from a long way away. However you can only request original material: that is records which are not yet online or on microfilm.

Visiting Kew

The reading rooms can seem daunting, but they are well organised. It is worth spending a few minutes talking to staff about what you are looking for, and checking out the reference books and other finding aids on the shelves. You may spend most of your time in the Open Reading Room which has all the records available on microfilm and online as well as an extensive library. However, you will need a reader's ticket to read original documents in the separate Document and Map and Large Document reading rooms.

The public areas are fully accessible for wheelchairs and there are facilities for the visually impaired and the deaf, although it is a good idea to get in contact before you travel so that everything can be made ready for your arrival. If you have difficulty lifting heavy documents (and many registers and volumes are bulky) please ask the staff and they will help carry them for you.

You are asked to take particular care of the records. They are unique. Advice about how to do this is available on The National Archives website and in the reading rooms. You are only allowed to take pencils and loose notes into the areas where you can read original documents. Laptops are welcome throughout the building (there is even free WiFi) and you are allowed to use digital cameras to take photographs of documents for your own use.

As well as the reading rooms, there is an excellent shop, a restaurant and an innovative museum showing just a few of the treasures you can find at Kew.

Visiting The National Archives is a fascinating experience and can be very rewarding. With a bit of luck you can find your ancestor quickly and easily. And there really is nothing that compares to handling a document that she handled or he signed.

Top tip

At Kew or not

The National Archives is the largest and most important archive in Britain, but it is not the only one. There are also separate national archives in Scotland and Northern Ireland (and, of course, the Republic of Ireland). And in England and Wales almost every county, and many large cities, has its own archive or record office caring for local records. In addition, many businesses, charities and universities also maintain archives. A full list can be found at **www.nationalarchives.gov.uk/archon**.

It can be a nightmare finding which records are held where. Fortunately help is at hand in the form of two complementary online databases – Access to Archives (A2A) at **www.nationalarchives. gov.uk/a2a** and the National Register of Archives at **www.nationalarchives.gov.uk/nra**. (For more about the Register see page 34). A2A is probably easier to use, but it is by no means comprehensive.

In addition, most library services provide a local studies room which will often have a lot of the basic genealogical resources on microfilm and disc as well as access to many online resources. They are also a good source for local newspapers. You can find them listed at **www.familia.org.uk**.

NB The National Archives does not hold BMD index books.

The New Kew

Using our exclusive step-by-step guide **Penny Law** shows you how to use the newly redesigned reading rooms and facilities at The National Archives

Over the past few months the public areas at Kew have been extensively remodelled. Whether you are a regular or a first timer to The National Archives, this guide will tell you what to expect.

At its heart lies the Open Reading Room on the First Floor, which allows readers to use digitised resources as well as those still available on microfilm without the need for a reader's ticket. It is here that you can talk to experts about your research or browse the indexes. If you need to look at original documents, such as ships' logs and most war diaries, you will need to obtain a Reader's Ticket and go into the Document Reading Room. Meanwhile maps and many pre-18th century records can be consulted in the Map and Large Document Reading Room on the Second Floor.

1. Your first port of call on entering The National Archives is the welcome desk. The staff here will give you a basic introduction to the Archives, although they no longer issue Reader's Tickets here. This is now done upstairs in the Open Reading Room.

2. Improved signposting of the reading rooms and facilities make it easier for readers to find their way round.

3. You only need a Reader's Ticket to read original documents. Getting a ticket is very straightforward, although you need to remember to bring two pieces of identification – one proving your identity, such as a bank card, and another proving your current address, like a recent utility bill. Tickets are valid for three years.

4. The National Archives has well over a hundred leaflets and research guides available in the reading rooms (and online) offering advice on the most common research topics.

5. At the end of the Open Reading Room, an extensive library, containing thousands of books on British history and other subjects, can be consulted by readers.

6. Throughout the reading rooms are many computer terminals which allow you to order documents, and search the online catalogue and digitised resources from The National Archives and elsewhere.

7. A number of indexes to many series of records are available on cards. However, they are slowly disappearing as entries from them are being added to the online catalogue.

8. This chart will show you where microfilms are located.

9. The National Archives holds many of the most popular record classes on microfilm. Once you know the reference number of the particular roll you need to look at, you simply take one of the blue "marker" boxes provided and put it in the place of the microfilm box you are taking out to use. When you are done with the microfilm you simply swap them back again.

10. Also available in the Open Reading Room is a set of class lists containing descriptions of the records at The National Archives. These volumes can be a useful supplement to the online catalogue.

11. There are always friendly, knowledgeable staff available to help readers with research queries or problems with the records.

12. The Open Reading Room has many printed reference books and guides to help researchers.

13. You can consult original documents in the Document Reading Room. They are placed in lockers or pigeon holes from where readers can collect them and take them to their allocated seat. Documents normally take up to 35 minutes to be delivered.

14. There is seating for nearly 700 people in the various reading rooms. There is also a new, separate area in which people who are working on projects together are allowed to look at and discuss documents.

17. A welcome resource is a coffee bar near the entrance to the building serving hot and cold drinks and snacks, as well as a restaurant serving more substantial dishes. The whole area has been opened-up and re-decorated making it the perfect place to relax at the end of a busy day trawling through the records in the Archives.

15. On the second floor we have an extensive map collection dating back to medieval times and varying from sets of Ordnance Survey maps to plans of royal palaces.

16. There is a large locker room on the ground floor where you can securely leave coats and any personal belongings. No bags are allowed to be taken into the Document Reading Room apart from clear plastic ones which are provided in the locker room.

Visiting The National Archives

The National Archives offers a unique record of the past. Its holdings cover the British Isles, the territories that formed the British Empire and the countries of the Commonwealth. Material varies from the Domesday Book to the most recent government papers. There are many records for family historians, including 19th and 20th century census returns, pre-1920 Army and Navy service records, and material relating to emigration and immigration.

Kew, Richmond, Surrey TW9 4DU; telephone; 020 8876 3444; website **www.nationalarchives.gov.uk**.

Reader's Tickets

You need a Reader's Ticket to look at original documents in the Document Reading Room or Map and Large Document Reading Room. You do not need a Reader's Ticket to use the Open Reading Room or the restaurant, cyber café, shop and museum. You should bring proof of identity and address with you in case you decide you need a ticket. It is possible to pre-register for a ticket at **www.nationalarchives.gov.uk/registration**.

You can use portable computers and digital cameras but not pens, coloured pencils or scanners, in the reading rooms.

WHO, WHERE AND WHEN

Melinda Haunton explains how the National Register of Archives can help family historians track down where records are held

Ever since it was established shortly after the Second World War, the National Register of Archives (NRA) has been amassing information on where historical documents are stored, and what they contain.

It can point you to archival collections relating to British history, not just in Britain but also in more than 45 countries overseas, including material held in national repositories, local record offices, small organisations and even in private hands.

All the researcher has to do to enter this internet treasure trove is click on The National Archives's website, **www.nationalarchives.gov.uk/nra**.

Because family history can be much more than a simple record of births, marriages and deaths, resources like the NRA allow you to discover a deeper, richer story. So as you start to move beyond the basics I recommend exploring to see what you can find. While you are unlikely to dig out direct information about your ancestors, the site can help in other ways. For instance, if your family were Nonconformists, the NRA can help you locate chapel records. Perhaps some

Below, Lord Henry Lennox is depicted in the *Illustrated London News*, cutting the first sod for the Midhurst to Chichester railway on 22 April 1865. Left, search results on the National Register of Archives site when you key in "Chichester" AND "Midhurst" AND "Railway".

forebears were involved in a local charity whose archives can be tracked down. Or your family were tenants on a major estate, where papers have survived.

Begin your search with the online indexes, which let you trawl a huge database to locate records for over 100,000 individuals, families, businesses and organisations. You can key in the name of a place, person, family or body that created the records.

For example, you can call up school records by keying in the school's name. You will then see a list of matching results, each of which relates to one or more surviving archive collections. This material is described, together with details about where it is held. The descriptions are brief, but should be sufficient to indicate whether the collection is likely to be relevant to your research.

If material is available in an online catalogue, such as Access to Archives, there is a link to the relevant website. Many original paper documents, for instance, can be found in the Open Reading Room at Kew. Your next step is to contact the archive which holds the material you need, using a link to ARCHON, The National Archives's online archival address book.

Find a place

The place search allows you to pinpoint all known archives relating to a specific location. This is particularly helpful if your family were long-term residents in a specific town or village and you want to explore potential connections, or you are researching a town's history.

For example, a simple search for Midhurst in Sussex turns up 25 record-creating bodies which relate to the town, from the local ironmongers to the parish charity. Each shows the record creator's name as a hyperlink, which you can click on for further information about what records survive. There is also a number in brackets, indicating how many collections exist. The full NRA entry will typically contain:

- The name of the individual, family, business or organisation that created the records.
- A short summary of the records, usually including covering dates of the collection.
- The location of the records (including a link to contact details for this repository).
- A record office reference number of the records.
- An NRA catalogue number.
- References to printed publications, surveys, guides and reports, available in the Open Reading Room at Kew.

A row of NRA catalogues in the Open Reading Room at Kew.

- Links which will take you to fuller online listings on sites like Access to Archives (A2A), Archives Network Wales or the Archives Hub.

The phrase "Annual return 2004", means we acquired the information through the annual *Accessions to Repositories* used to update the NRA every year. However, you should not assume that such collections are accessible immediately. This pattern of information may be repeated if various different collections of records survive for a particular person, family or corporate body. This can be very helpful in tracking down collections which are not in the most obvious places.

For example, when you look for information on the records of the Chichester and Midhurst Railway, you will find a few documents are held by West Sussex Record Office, the local archive; but minute books from between 1864 and 1871 are at The National Archives in series RAIL 115.

Occasionally you will find entries where the location is given as "private". Click on this word

Diss Mere, Norfolk, taken in 1866, one of many images held by Norfolk and Norwich Millennium Library.

Norfolk County Council Library & Information Service

for further information about who to contact for more details. A local archive may be able to put you in touch with the owner, or you may need to give a few days' notice before consulting the records. Although some material is held by people who are not able to make it fully available to the public, this is relatively uncommon. Many owners will do everything possible to help you.

Trace a person

If you are very lucky, you may discover some relevant information by searching for the name of an individual. Most people who leave a significant collection of papers are prominent in some area of public life. So if you have a famous or notable ancestor, it is certainly worth checking to see whether they left anything for posterity.

Nevertheless, some records of "ordinary" people are on file. Individuals whose papers survive include: a Mrs Baldwin, who visited soldiers in hospital in North London during the First World War; Ernie Trory, who was a Brighton Communist in the 1930s; and Annie Best, of Red Rice, Upper Clatford, who left a hunting diary for 1896.

This means it is always worth checking your family name(s) in the person search – just don't be too disappointed if you don't score a result.

Find a family

Again, it tends to be comparatively well-known families who left a significant collection of papers for later generations.

However, the index is particularly useful in tracking down records of landed families. If you know your ancestors were tenants of a particular family, you can simply search for surviving estate material by the family name. Alternatively, if you suspect they were tenants but do not know the name of the family concerned, you can do an advanced search

which will locate families with estates in the area that interests you.

For example, in Diss, on the Norfolk-Suffolk border, the area from which my own family originates, six local landed families left substantial records. They included the Collingwoods, whose papers are held at Northumberland Record Office, and the Marshams, Earls of Romney, whose papers are mainly at the Centre for Kentish Studies in Maidstone. Most of the other relevant records are either in Norfolk Record Office or the Ipswich branch of Suffolk Record Office, but a few are in Berkshire and Oxford. A search of just Norfolk would not necessarily bring up this geographical scattering of documents.

Gather group papers

The corporate name search is used to hunt for record-creating bodies which are neither people nor families – essentially any business or organisation. There are also oddities that do not fit neatly into any category, but which still created important record series, such as tithes, elections, ships and commons. You can simply search for these by name on the main screen, or again, choose to search in more detail.

For example, if you know your family farmed in Devon, but are not sure of the farm name, you can search by category "Agriculture, forestry and fisheries", sub-sector "farmers and growers", specifying the county of Devon. You will find 59 results – Devonian farmers through the ages whose records have survived.

Tantalisingly, there are 10 anonymous sets of records for Devon farms. It can be difficult for an archivist to identify a business by name if all that survive are a few documents. So if your ancestors farmed in Culm Davy around 1800, Devon Record Office holds a set of accounts from an unknown farm there, and it just might be a lost part of your family history!

A typical Irish landscape in County Cork.

Tracing *your* Irish ancestors

Start researching your family in Ireland as **Ian Maxwell** takes you on a journey through the basic official records

"**The danger in tracing your family tree,**" George Bernard Shaw once declared, "**is that you may find an ancestor hanging from a branch, either by his neck or by his tail.**"

Happily, more than 84,000 visitors who come to Ireland each year are prepared to take the risk, with roots tourism now giving a big boost to the Irish economy.

Irish ancestral research is hampered by the destruction of many major record collections, so you will have to make greater use of church

records, school registers, and land and valuation records than in England, Scotland or Wales. Nevertheless, with diligence, family historians should be able to trace their roots to the beginning of the 19th century, while a lucky few may be able to go back even further than the early 17th century.

To make best use of the records it is essential to know where your ancestors lived in Ireland. Linking your family to a county is a great help, but you really need to identify their parish or townland (one of the most ancient divisions in the country and the most basic unit of local government until the 20th century), of origin. If you only know the county, try one of Ireland's county-based heritage centres. Established as part of the Irish Genealogical Project, which aims to create a comprehensive genealogical database for the entire island of Ireland, each centre indexes and computerises records of a particular county, or in some cases two counties. Staff will search their databases for a fee.

Census returns

British genealogists often start their research with census returns, which basically give a head count of every person living in the country. The first properly organised census in Ireland took place in 1821, and thereafter, with some exceptions, one was taken every 10 years. Unfortunately, returns from 1821 to 1851 were lost when the Public Record Office in Dublin was destroyed in 1922, while those from 1861 to 1891 were pulped into waste paper during the First World War. The earliest surviving complete censuses covering the whole of Ireland are therefore those of 1901 and 1911. These should be the first records consulted by anyone still living in Ireland, or those whose ancestors emigrated subsequent to or shortly before these dates.

The censuses provide: ages and relationships of family members, occupations, religious denominations, counties of birth and, in the case of the 1911 forms, number of years married.

You can see the original returns for 1901 at the National Archives in Dublin, or view microfilm copies at the Public Record Office of Northern Ireland (PRONI). The 1911 census is not yet available at PRONI because of the 100-year rule on access in the United Kingdom, but the original census returns can be viewed at the National Archives in Dublin. Both are slowly being digitised and placed online at **www.census.nationalarchives.ie**. This is a free service. At present only the 1911 records

for Dublin are available, although those for counties Kerry, Antrim, Down, Donegal and Cork are due to be added shortly.

Property valuations

The loss of so much 19th century census material means the family historian must use the two great property valuations of that century – the Tithe (church tax) Applotment Books, compiled between the 1820s and 30s, and Griffith's Primary Valuation, compiled between 1848 and 1864.

Tithe applotment books are unique records, giving details of land occupation and valuations for individual holdings prior to the devastation of the Great Famine, and the resultant mass emigration. However, landless labourers, weavers and all purely urban dwellers are not included.

The National Archives in Dublin, holds a tithe manuscript book for almost every parish in the 26 counties of the Republic of Ireland – totalling over 2,000. These are also available on microfilm at the National Library and the Gilbert Library in Dublin. Northern Ireland's 270-plus volumes for Northern Ireland are held by PRONI.

The only 19th century sources listing all householders in Ireland are the land valuation records, which date from the mid-1800s. The first valuation, carried out in the 1830s, can be an important source. Although only a few householders were named in rural areas – usually the gentry or better class tenant farmers – in towns, many more properties were substantial enough to reach the valuation of £3, so a larger number are recorded.

By contrast, the 1848 to 1864 valuation gives a complete list of occupiers of land, tenements and houses. This Primary Valuation of Ireland, better known as Griffith's Valuation

A tithe applotment book for Tullynamulion township, Connor Parish, County Antrim.
Derry Genealogical Centre

after Richard Griffith, the Commissioner of Valuation, was made to determine how much tax or rates each person should pay towards supporting the poor and destitute in each poor law union. Details include:

- the townland
- name of the householder or leaseholder
- who the property was leased from
- description of the property
- its acreage
- valuation of the land and buildings

This can be a useful source for someone with emigrant ancestors as it was largely complete for the South and West of the

FIVE TIPS FOR USING THE 1911 AND 1901 IRISH CENSUS

1. The Irish 1911 Census for Dublin is now available online.

2. Like other censuses for elsewhere in the British Isles you can search by name.

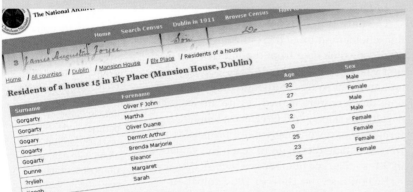

3. A transcript gives brief details of everybody in the household on census night.

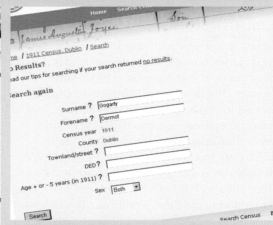

4. You can also search by place. If you know the name of the street (and ideally the house number) where an ancestor lived this can sometimes be easier than searching by their surname.

5. There are a number of different schedules you can download for each house, but the most useful is the household return (Form A).

country before mass emigrations following the Great Famine after 1845.

The one million-plus names in the valuation can now be searched on Family Tree Maker's CD-ROM, Index to Griffith's Valuation. It is also available free of charge online at **http://griffiths.askaboutireland.ie**. In addition, you can use the website to identify the land that your ancestor owned on Ordnance Survey maps of the period.

Life events

State registration of all births, deaths and marriages began in Ireland on 1 January 1864. Non-Catholic marriages, including Protestant and Jewish marriages, as well as those conducted in a government registry office, had already been required to be registered from 1 April 1845.

The General Register Office (*Oifig An Ard-Chlaraitheora*) is the civil repository for records relating to births, deaths and marriages in the Republic of Ireland.

The General Register Office (GRO) in Belfast holds the original birth and death registers recorded by the local district registrars for Northern Ireland from 1864. Although indexes to civil marriage registers from 1845 for Northern Ireland are available at the GRO, original registers are located in district registrars' offices at local councils. Indexes can be searched for a fee. To obtain the full information contained in the register entry you will need to purchase a print-out or certificate.

Ironically, the Mormon Church has copied almost all the civil registers and indexes, which can be accessed free of charge at any of its family history centres.

For information on births, deaths and marriages prior to civil registration, researchers need to consult church registers kept by the various religious denominations. There was a legal obligation for the Church of Ireland to keep records from 1634, although many rural parishes did not start to keep detailed records until the mid-18th century. However, Church of Ireland records generally start much earlier than those of other Protestant denominations and the Roman Catholic Church.

In 1876 over 1,000 records were deposited in the Public Record Office. Many were subsequently destroyed in the fire of 1922. Surviving registers, some 630 in number, are either held by the parish, at the National Archives or PRONI, or with the Representative Church Library in Dublin.

Roman Catholicism is, of course, the overwhelmingly predominate creed in Ireland. Starting dates for Catholic parish records vary; the oldest were produced in the cities with some dating back to the late 18th century. Copies of most Catholic parish registers are held on microfilm in the National Library of Ireland, with copies of those for Northern counties held by PRONI. The largest collection of records from a wide variety of Protestant denominations, including Presbyterian and Methodist, are also held by PRONI, although some – particularly Baptist records – still remain in local custody.

Wills

Once an ancestor's date of death has been discovered, it is worth finding out whether they left a will. Prior to 1858 the Church of Ireland was responsible for administering all testamentary affairs via Ecclesiastical or Consistorial Courts in each diocese. After that date such matters came under civil jurisdiction.

Wills contain not only the name, address and occupation of the testator, but also details of the larger family network, such as cousins and nephews. Many wills also include the addresses and occupations of the beneficiaries, witnesses and executors.

Unfortunately most original wills made before 1858 were lost in the 1922 fire. However, bound printed and manuscript indexes are available at the Irish National Archives and at PRONI. Later wills were also destroyed in 1922, but transcript copies survived, and are available in Dublin and Belfast on microfilm for the period 1858 to 1900.

Schools

Although state-run education was not established in Ireland until 1831, the surviving records can be an invaluable source for the family historian. The attendance registers contain information that can compensate for the lack of 19th century census records.

The earliest registers date from the 1860s. They record:
■ full name of the pupil, date of birth (or age of entry)
■ religion
■ father's address and occupation
■ details of attendance and academic progress
■ any school previously attended

A space provided for general comments might tell you where a child went to work afterwards or whether he/she emigrated.

A significant proportion of National School Registers are available at PRONI or the National Archives in Dublin.

USEFUL ADDRESSES

NORTHERN IRELAND

Public Record Office of Northern Ireland, 66 Balmoral Avenue, Belfast, BT9 6NY; 028 9025 5905; **www.proni.gov.uk**. During 2010 the Office will be moving to a new home in central Belfast and services may be disrupted during the move. You should check before you visit.

Belfast Ulster and Irish Studies Library at Belfast Central Library, Royal Avenue Belfast BT1 1EA; 028 9050 9199; **www.ni-libraries.net**

Linenhall Library, 17 Donegall Square North, Belfast BT1 5GB; 028 9032 1707; **www.linenhall.com**

General Register Office, Oxford House, 49/55 Chichester Street, Belfast BT1 4HL; 028 9025 2000; **www.groni.gov.uk**

REPUBLIC OF IRELAND

National Archives of Ireland, Bishop Street, Dublin 8; 00353 1 407 2300; **www.national archives.ie**

Genealogy Advisory Service at the National Library of Ireland, Kildare Streeet, Dublin 2; 00353 1 603 0230; **www.nli.ie**

General Register Office, Convent Road, Roscommon, 00353 9 066 32900; **www.groireland.ie** Public search room, Joyce House, 8–11 Lombard Street, Dublin 8; 00353 1 671 1000

For details of the 33 local Heritage Centres in Ireland visit **www. irishgenealogy.ie**.

RESEARCHING THE SCOTS

David McVey considers the resources available for researching Scottish ancestors online

The Scots get around. Tens of millions of people all over the world have some form of Scottish ancestry. There are an estimated five million in Canada alone, (the same as the population of modern Scotland), an estimated two million in England and Wales, and 21 million scattered across the United States.

It's quite likely that, whoever you are and wherever you're from, as you research your family history you'll hit upon a Scottish connection.

Happily, there are now plentiful web resources to help you begin your investigations at home.

The first stop, inevitably, is the groundbreaking ScotlandsPeople website (**www.scotlandspeople.gov.uk**).

The site has digitised records for:

■ statutory records of births, marriages and deaths for the years after 1855
■ parish records for 1854 and earlier
■ 1841–1901 census records
■ pre-1901 wills and testaments

Searching these records is free, but for full access and downloading rights you'll need to purchase online credits. However, the costs aren't onerous for digitised documents that put you within touching distance of your family's past.

The website of the General Register Office for Scotland (**www.gro-scotland.gov.uk**) has advice about using ScotlandsPeople, some very useful tips for family research in Scotland, and guidelines on how to go about obtaining information from censuses more recent than those available on ScotlandsPeople.

Along the same lines is the National Archive of Scotland (NAS) website (**www.nas.gov.uk**) which is a goldmine of fascinating resources, with a useful search facility to help you identify relevant bits of the main collections. The Archive's specialist family history page can be found at **www.nas.gov.uk/familyhistory**. This gives some valuable specific advice for genealogical research with a Scottish accent.

Family historians often find older styles of handwriting somewhat discouraging, and if you are used to English historical documents, you will notice that Scottish handwriting has

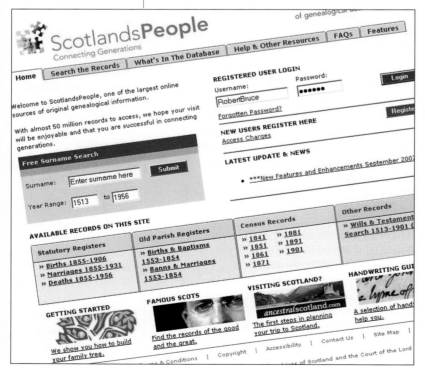

its own unique features. And that's before you factor in words and phrases peculiar to the Scottish legal system. I've stared blankly at documents as recent as the late 18th century that refuse to give up their secrets.

Help is available at a site run by the NAS which offers online tutorials in deciphering older Scottish handwriting at **www.scottishhandwriting.com**.

These minutes from Aberlour Kirk session in 1657 demonstrate how tricky it can be to decipher old Scottish handwriting.

On reflection, this might be a good site to use before you start downloading documents from ScotlandsPeople.

An avenue of research unique to Scotland is, of course, the clan system. You don't have to have any tangible recent Highlands and Islands family heritage to end up researching it; I'm from a

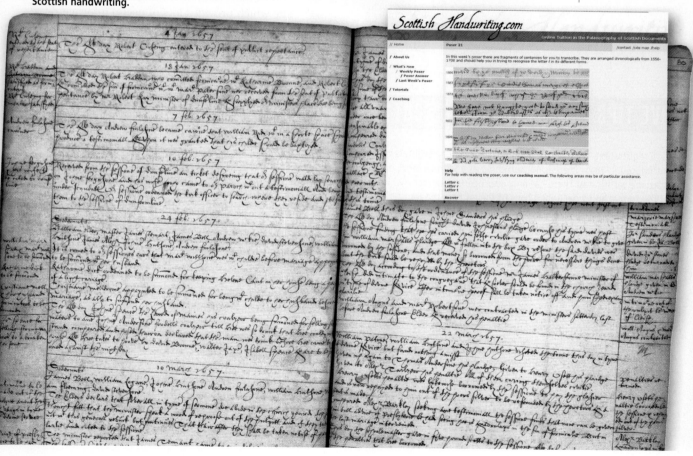

During 2009, the Homecoming Scotland festival will offer an extensive programme of exciting and inspirational events and activities marking the 250th anniversary of the birth of Scotland's most famous son Robbie Burns. Perhaps the most exciting event for people with Scots ancestry is the world's largest ever clan gathering, which will take place in late July in Edinburgh. Not only can you experience the World Highland Games championship at Holyrood Park, but ancestral Scots can join thousands of other proud ancestral Scots in the clan parade up the length of the historic Royal Mile, before attending an amazing spectacular at the Clan Pageant on the esplanade of Edinburgh Castle. Another highlight is the International Genealogy Festival (and Ceilidh) at Glasgow's University of Strathclyde also in late July.

For more about the celebrations visit **www.homecomingscotland2009.com**.

long-standing urban West Scotland background, but my surname is, nonetheless, Highland (the McVeys were a sept of the Macleans of Duart).

Many of the websites can be less than rigorous or authoritative, run by informal clan societies or individual enthusiasts, and discernment is needed. Let's suppose you're a former English football manager with the surname McClaren and you want to investigate your Highland roots. You could pop into a site such as **www.ancestralscotland.com** where a quick surname search will lead you to places where McClarens were recorded as living in the 1881 census. A clan search will provide a wee potted history and even a picture of an associated tartan.

Some sites are operated by the Highland diaspora. For example, this American one for those with an interest in Clan MacLaren: **www.clanmaclarenna.org**.

If you choose to carry out a web search for clan sites related to your own family name, make sure you exercise caution.

And of course there are lots of sites if you are searching a particular area. We'll use Glasgow as an example partly because, as the most populous city in Scotland, it's very likely to crop up in your researches, and also because everybody ought to have Glasgow connections (although I might be biased). One site which provides lots of useful information is **www.familia.org.uk/services/scotland/glasgow.html**.

Similarly, Glasgow's local family history

FIVE TIPS FOR RESEARCHING SCOTTISH FAMILY HISTORY

1 Civil registration – a nationwide system of Statutory Registers was introduced in 1855. There is no such thing as a Scottish birth, death or marriage certificates. There has only ever been an extract – which is what the formal and legally valid copy of the entry in the register of births, or marriages, or deaths is called. That said, the term certificate is widely used, even by the General Register Office for Scotland!

2 Birth, marriage and death extracts are more informative than their equivalents in England and Wales. Birth extracts give the place and date of the marriage of the parents. Those for marriages give the names of both parents of the bride and groom, including the mothers' maiden names. Ones for deaths give the names of both parents of the deceased, including the maiden name of the mother; as well as the marital status and names of all spouses of the deceased (as long as the informant knew) .

3 Census records begin in 1841 and are almost identical to the English ones. The latest ones available are for 1901. As well as being available on the ScotlandsPeople website, transcripts can also be found at **www.ancestry.co.uk**.

4 Before 1855 the best source are Old Parish Registers (OPR), which record baptisms and marriages (but rarely burials). Unfortunately they are incomplete, difficult to use and each one varies enormously in the information given. They begin in 1553, but most date from the late 18th century and later. Registration was costly and unpopular, so many people did not bother to register events at all. And, as in England, members of Nonconformist denominations increasingly preferred to register events in their own churches and chapels.

5 Not everything is in Edinburgh. The Scottish Archive Network website at **www.scan.org.uk** allows you to search the electronic catalogues of more than 50 Scottish archives with over 20,000 collections of historical records. Partners involved in the project include the National Archives of Scotland, the National Library of Scotland, Scottish Screen Archive, and smaller bodies like the Scottish Jewish Archives Centre and the Royal College of Nursing archives.

Crown Copyright General Register Office for Scotland

society has a fascinating site packed with advice and resources (**www.gwsfhs.org.uk**).

The relevant local authority site for your search area is also worth a look. That of the Glasgow City Council (**www.glasgow.gov.uk/en/Visitors/ FamilyHistory**) offers a number of useful links, including the resources and archives of the city's famous Mitchell Library.

Again, bear in mind that these locally-based resources for Glasgow are mirrored in many other parts of the country. Another example is the Highland Council service (**www.highland.gov.uk/leisureandtourism/ what-to-see/archives/ highlandcouncilarchives**).

I've chosen to mention this one because Highland Council is creating a new Highland Archive Centre in Inverness which will have a dedicated Family History Centre within its walls. Hopefully, digitisations will be offered online once the centre is up and running in 2009.

If you uncover family history connections in Scotland, no doubt you'll want to visit the

SCOTTISH GENEALOGICAL SOCIETY

Founded in 1953 the Scottish Genealogical Society exists to serve everyone who has an interest in Scottish genealogy. At the heart of their activities is their library and family history centre which lies in the shadows of Edinburgh Castle. Over the years the Society has built up a diverse, fascinating and truly unique collection of books and manuscripts including reference books and directories, biographies, topographies, gazetteers, trades and profession lists, general Scottish history, peerage, heraldry, school and university rolls, and individual family collections, both published and unpublished. Books and manuscripts relating to Scottish families in other countries around the world have also been donated to the library. Over the years, members and friends have sent copies of their pedigrees, family histories and research notes etc and these have all been meticulously indexed by surname in the Family History Index.

The Index has over 2,500 separate files deposited by researchers with the Society over a period of almost 50 years. Each file contains research on a specific family or number of families, and there may be a number of files for a given family. The files range in size from one page to substantial family histories running to tens or even hundreds of pages. They may take the form of research notes, random jottings, family group sheets, pedigree charts, family trees, original documents, transcripts, newspaper cuttings, photographs or fully written up histories.

The Scottish Genealogy Society, 15 Victoria Terrace, Edinburgh EH1 2JL; telephone 0131 220 3677; **www.scotsgenealogy.com**.

country and check out the sites and sources in person. You'll be made very welcome if you do. But you might first want to call in at **www.ancestralscotland.com** which combines genealogical help with advice for pilgrims to the country. However, the various web resources available to you mean that you can do a lot of the hard work before you go and, at the very least, target your hands-on research more effectively.

An extract from the 1892 deaths register for the district of Rutherglen in Lanarkshire.

British soldiers and sailors landing on a heavily defended beach near Aboukir in 1801 during the Napoleonic Wars.

Military records
Before 1913

During the 18th and 19th centuries tens of thousands of men served in the armed forces. **Simon Fowler** lines up the facts for family historians

Some of the most popular records at The National Archives relate to the Army and the Navy. If your ancestors served in the forces before 1913 then you are in luck, because the records they left behind can be very informative, particularly for the Army. There are a few records going back to the 1660s, but the bulk start a century later.

Britain's armed services have always been small. In 1899, at the height of the nation's imperial power, there were just 180,000 other ranks and officers in the Army and 93,000 ratings and officers in the Navy. The Army alternated between service in the Britain Isles and tours of duty in the Empire, particularly India. In addition the Government of India

maintained its own army. But the real defensive force was the Royal Navy. According to the original 18th century Articles of War: "It is upon the Navy that under the good providence of God the wealth, the prosperity and peace of these Islands and of the Empire do mainly depend."

As ever, the more information you have before you start, the easier your search will be. In particular you must have an idea of which unit a man served with: that is a regiment or corps in the Army, or ship in the Navy. This is very important if you are researching men who left the forces before the mid-19th century, as service records were then largely organised by unit.

It is also important to know whether they were officers or ordinary soldiers and sailors, as the records are very different. If you are not sure, check the Army or Navy Lists, which list all officers; The National Archives has a complete set. Some libraries also have copies, and you may occasionally find digitised versions online.

GOING FOR A SOLDIER

To understand how your soldier ancestor fitted into the scheme of things, you need to have a grasp of how the Army is organised. The most important unit has traditionally been the regiment for the infantry, guards and cavalry, and the corps for artillerymen and engineers. Up until the mid-18th century, regiments might be raised for a particular campaign, then disbanded; after 1760 regiments became more permanent so their history is easier to follow. A regiment normally consisted of one or two battalions, each comprising perhaps 1,000 men. One battalion was generally stationed abroad while the other was based in Britain, recruiting and training troops.

Traditionally, other ranks enlisted for 21 years, but in the 1870s this was cut to six years in an attempt to make the Army more attractive to potential recruits. Until the 1860s desertion was common, as men found they could not endure the harsh conditions.

In the Army, barracks were overcrowded and squalid, and the diet meagre. During the 1850s, for example, the standard diet consisted of a daily ration of a pound of bread, eaten at breakfast with coffee, and three quarters of a pound of meat boiled for midday dinner in large coppers in cookhouses. Life was made bearable by companionship and drink; few soldiers managed to remain undisciplined for drunkenness during their service. However, under pressure from civilian groups and the difficulties of recruiting sufficient men, conditions began to improve from the 1860s.

Traditionally soldiers came from the poorest strata of society, while their officers came from the landed gentry. During the Napoleonic Wars, the Duke of Wellington famously described his troops as being the "scum of the earth". He then went on: "People talk of their enlisting from fine military feeling – all stuff – no such thing. Some of men enlist from having got bastard children – some for minor offences – many more for drink; it is really a wonder that we should make them the fine fellows they are."

Officers were largely from the landed classes, who had a private income to pay for entertaining and the exotic uniforms. Before the First World War, perhaps four or five officers each year were promoted from the ranks, the most famous of whom was William Robertson who joined the Lincolnshire Regiment as a private in the 1870s and rose to the rank of Field Marshal – the first man to do so. Officers were generally poorly trained, learning their military skills during colonial campaigns, but at the end of the 19th century the Army Staff College was beginning to make them more professional.

Staff officers during the Crimean War.

TOP TIPS

BY SEA BY LAND

The first marines – that is soldiers who served on board naval ships – were recruited in 1664. The greatest of their earliest achievements was in 1704 when the British attacked the Rock of Gibraltar: marines prevented Spanish reinforcements reaching the fortress. Today the Royal Marines display only one battle honour – Gibraltar. They were granted the Royal prefix in 1802.

In 1755, 50 new companies of marines were raised, grouped into three divisions – Chatham, Plymouth and Portsmouth. A fourth division existed at Woolwich between 1805 and 1869.

In 1804 marine companies of artillery were created becoming a distinct division in 1859, as the Royal Marine Artillery. They were nicknamed the "Blue Marines" from the uniform worn. In 1855 the infantry companies were designated the title of the Royal Marine Light Infantry (or "Red Marines"). They came together again in 1923.

As with the Army and Navy, the vast majority of records are at The National Archives. Service records for officers are in series ADM 196 (from 1796, although they are incomplete before 1837) and they appear in both the Army and Navy Lists. They are available online at **www.nationalarchives.gov.uk/documentsonline**.

Service records for other ranks are in series ADM 159 with attestation papers in ADM 157 and description books in ADM 158. Records are arranged by division, although there are surname indexes in ADM 313 which provide this information.

The National Army Museum and regimental museums may on occasion be able to help with soldiers and, particularly, officers. Similarly, the National Maritime Museum and the Royal Naval Museum may have information on naval officers and ratings.

The Society of Genealogists' library has a fair collection of printed material, such as medal rolls, casualty lists, and biographies for both services.

The *Family and Local History Handbook* contains addresses for most regimental museums and they are also available online at **www.army museums.org.uk**.

The records

Unless otherwise indicated, the records described below are only at The National Archives at Kew. Staff will direct you to the relevant documents.

OFFICERS:

Published lists – every officer is named in the *Army Lists*. You should be able to find details of promotions; the unit he served with; and sometimes brief details of the campaigns in which he fought. From 1839 there's a rival *Hart's Army List*, which also contains biographical information. As well as sets at The National Archives, some copies have been scanned and are available online or on CD.

Service records – there are five series which may contain material. A comprehensive card index indicates which records are held where in the reading rooms.

Commissions – correspondence about the purchase and sale of commissions between 1793 and 1871 contains a lot of valuable genealogical material.

Pensions – there are registers and correspondence about the payment of pensions up to 1921, including some records concerning pensions paid to widows and children.

OTHER RANKS

Service records – there are two series of records, but only for men who survived to receive a pension. Before 1883 records are arranged by regiment, although a name index to records before 1854 is online at **www.nationalarchives.gov.uk/catalogue**. The documents indicate when and where a man served; promotions; disciplinary offences (generally drunkenness, desertion or failure to obey orders); place and age on enlistment; reason for discharge; and they sometimes list wives and children.

Muster rolls – compiled monthly, these list every man in a regiment (including officers). They indicate a man's pay, offences committed during the previous month and location of regiment. They begin in 1732 and end in 1898.

Pensions – men who left the Army after serving their time, or as the result of wounds, were entitled to a pension from Chelsea

SAILOR AHOY!

Conditions in the Royal Navy were no better than in the Army. Until the 1850s, when a permanent career structure was introduced, men signed on for a particular voyage, so might well serve on both Royal Navy and merchant ships. And officers could spend much of their time ashore on half pay, waiting for a posting.

There was little chance of promotion, while being commissioned as an officer was a very rare occurrence. The gulf between officer and men was every bit as great as in the Army. Again, this was largely the result of the different social backgrounds – the aristocracy and middle classes for officers and the working class for ratings.

It is fair to say that the Navy's methods during the Napoleonic wars had changed so little over the previous two centuries that a sailor who had fought against the Spanish Armada in 1588, would have noticed little difference at the Battle of Trafalgar. This changed during the 19th century, when equipment and tactics were revolutionised: steam replaced wind-power; the screw propeller supplanted the sail; bigger and better guns were introduced; and wireless telegraphy transformed how ships communicated.

Conditions for ratings also gradually improved. Under Nelson, standard rations were based on hard ship's biscuits and salt beef and pork, all of which could be years old, while breakfast consisted of a mixture of oatmeal and molasses, known as "burgoo". Fresh vegetables and fruit were provided to counteract scurvy, but could be hard to come by on long missions in foreign waters. However, by the First World War larger ships might even have their own bakeries.

The records

OFFICERS

All naval officers appear in the *Navy List*, from which it is possible to trace

The discharge document for Rifleman Benjamin Harris in 1814. Harris was the model for Richard Sharpe in the television series and books by Bernard Cornwell.

Medals – there are medal rolls for campaigns from the Battle of Waterloo onwards, listing both officers and other ranks entitled to medals. For more, see our article on page 58.

For more, see our article on page 58.

TAKING IT FURTHER

There are a number of excellent books on tracing naval and military servicemen:

Richard Brooks and Matthew Little, *Royal Marine Ancestors* (Pen & Sword, 2008)

Ken Divall, *My Ancestor was a Royal Marine* (Society of Genealogists, 2007)

Simon Fowler, *A Guide to Military History on the Internet* (Pen & Sword, 2007)

Simon Fowler, *Tracing Your Army Ancestors* (Pen & Sword, 2006)

Bruno Pappalardo, *Tracing Your Naval Ancestors* (The National Archives, 2003)

William Spencer, *Army Records: a guide for family historians* (The National Archives, 2008)

William Spencer, *Medals: the researcher's guide* (The National Archives, 2008)

Useful addresses

National Army Museum, Royal Hospital Road, London SW3 47DX; telephone 020 7773 0717; **www.national-army-museum.ac.uk**

Maritime Research Centre, National Maritime Museum, Greenwich London SE10 9NF; telephone 020 8312 6516; **www.nmm.ac.uk**

Royal Naval Museum, HM Base (PP66), Main Road, Portsmouth PO1 3HN; **www.royalnavalmuseum.org/research.htm**

Society of Genealogists, 14 Charterhouse Buildings, Goswell Rd, London EC1M 7BA; telephone 029 7251 8799; **www.sog.org.uk**

Hospital. Most men were out-pensioners, receiving a pension at home. There are a variety of records listing pensions paid.

promotions and ships served on. There are also service records for men after 1840, although some retrospective entries date back to 1756. These records will give you the ships served on, promotions, some personal details and those of any spouse. An interesting source is passing certificates, which were issued to prove qualifications of officers. They give service and some personal details. You can view an incomplete list of officers since 1660 at **www.navylist.org**. Many service records are also now available online at **www.nationalarchives.gov.uk/documentsonline**.

Other ranks

Before 1853 there are no service records for ratings. Men were discharged at the end of each voyage, so there is no continuity of service. There are however three potential hunting places:

■ For men who retired with a pension between 1802 and 1894, try the certificates of service, which list the ships served on and dates of service.

■ Ships' muster and pay books will tell you when he enlisted, his age and place of birth.

■ Ships' logbooks may also help, and certainly provide more information on the voyages themselves.

After 1853 a new series of continuous service engagement were introduced, which formed the basis of service records until 1923. After 1894, however, you will have to know which specialist branch he served with. You should be able to find dates of entry and discharge, ships served on, promotions, disciplinary records and some personal details. They are largely available online at **www.nationalarchives.gov.uk/documentsonline**.

Medal rolls list gallantry and campaign medals awarded to both officers and ratings.

The survey return of 1817 for George Cannings, who was a lieutenant on HMS *Achilles* at the Battle of Trafalgar.

Tracing those who served during the
First World War

Because of its sheer scale, the First World War affected virtually every family in the United Kingdom. **Michael Paterson** shows how to trace ancestors who were in the Forces

Previous conflicts had taken place in distant parts of the world, and largely only involved Britain's small, professional armed forces, but the First World War was different. At first, recruiting volunteers was sufficient to provide the vast numbers required to expand the Army. As the war went on, however, this supply of manpower proved inadequate and at the beginning of 1916, in what was an unprecedented measure for Britain, conscription was introduced. In total, 5,704,400 men served during the war.

Meanwhile, places vacated by young men in the civilian workforce had to be filled by those too old or too young to fight, or by women, who made a significant contribution in commerce, industry, transport, and even in the armed services themselves.

Civilians not only participated in the war effort – often in some minor way, such as knitting scarves for the troops, or collecting scrap metal – but also shared some of the dangers. Over a thousand were killed in German air raids.

While the Western Front in Northern France and Belgium is the most familiar setting, but the war spread across the globe, Britain's armies also fought in Italy, Turkey, Mesopotamia (present-day Iraq), Salonika, Palestine, Africa and even China. The Royal Navy saw action in the North Sea and in the North and South Atlantic.

In all, 702,410 British service personnel were killed, along with around 206,000 troops from the Empire.

Despite the Armistice in November 1918, there was no clear-cut end to the conflict. Although hundreds of thousands of men were quickly demobilised, many others remained in uniform as the Government sought to deal with post-war problems, such as the occupation and policing of former enemy territories in Germany, Africa and the Middle East, the anti-Bolshevik intervention in Russia, and disturbances in Ireland.

HOW TO START YOUR RESEARCH

Your first step is to find out:
- Which branch of service your ancestor belonged to
- Whether he was an officer or "other rank" (this term encompasses all ranks from Private to Warrant Officer)
- Which regiment or corps he belonged to, and also his battalion

This last piece of information is especially important. A single infantry regiment might have 25 or 30 battalions, which could have served in places as disparate as Flanders, Egypt and India (the same is true of other formations, such as Royal Artillery batteries, brigades and companies). So finding the regiment to which your relation belonged may only be the beginning. Furthermore, a soldier might not have stayed in the same unit for the whole of his career. For a host of reasons, men transferred to other formations, particularly the Royal Air Force when it was created in April 1918.

As with other family history research projects, first look around your home for any clues, or papers kept by members of your family. There could be a photo of a man in uniform whose cap badge will identify his unit. He may have sent home greetings cards decorated with insignia, or commemorating particular events. His medals will be engraved with name, rank, number and unit. If he did not survive the war a bronze plaque (known as a Dead Man's Penny) will have been sent to his next of kin. Make a list of details provided by such keepsakes, perhaps creating a file of photocopied pictures and documents to take with you on visits to archives.

CASUALTY RECORDS

One of the first aspects you will discover is that soldiers who died are easier to trace than those who survived. Here are some starting points for your search if you know, or suspect, that a relative was killed.

- Look up the name on the Debt of Honour on the Commonwealth War Graves Commission website (**www.cwgc.org**). Since 1917 the Commission has been caring for military cemeteries all over the world. While other sites may deal with only a single service, the Commission's database covers all three – as well as merchant sailors and civilians on active service abroad. By entering a name you will be able to discover the man's rank, unit, date of death and the place where he is buried or commemorated. You may also find mention of his next of kin. The Western Front in particular is dotted with military cemeteries, some of which are immense. If you want to visit a grave, this website can save a good deal of time and trouble by providing an exact location.
- The *Soldiers died in the Great War* index is available both as a series of 81 published volumes – which you may well find in a large reference library – and as a CD-ROM, issued by Naval and Military Press. It can be consulted online, on a pay-per-view basis, at **www.military-genealogy.com**, **www.findmypast.com** and **www.familyrelatives.com**.

Identifying the cap badge on a photograph will identify his unit. In this case the badge is of the Durham Light Infantry.

During World War One, all the next of kin of Empire service personnel who lost their lives as a result of the war, were presented with a memorial plaque and commemorative scroll from the King and country. The plaques were cast in bronze and were approximately five inches in diameter. On the plaque itself no rank was recorded as the intention was to show equality in their sacrifice. It was known as a "Dead Man's Penny".

Casualty Form – Active Service for Horace Sydney Dickens. It shows he was first wounded in action some two months before his death on 27 July 1916 at Longueval. The chaos of the battle is starkly revealed in the notes: first he is recorded as 'Missing' and then 'Regarded for official purposes as having died on or since' that date.

Unusually – but deliberately – it is more forthcoming about other ranks than officers.

Information available on each man varies, but you should be able to discover where he was born, where he lived and where he enlisted. It should also give the rough cause of death: killed in action, died of wounds or died from natural causes. These details can sometimes be linked to his place of burial. A death from wounds would explain why he is buried in a rear area cemetery – no doubt close to a hospital or casualty clearing station – rather than near the battlefield on which he fought.

■ War memorials are another useful source. In the years following the Armistice, nearly 50,000 were built and dedicated to the fallen. These were by no means all stone structures; they might be in the form of a wall plaque, a tree, or some public amenity such as a park. Memorials were not only raised by communities – companies, schools, sports clubs and all manner of other organisations had their own, which sometimes provide details not recorded elsewhere.

You can consult the United Kingdom National Inventory of War Memorials at **www.ukniwm.org.uk**. It should be stressed that this will not list the individuals on a particular memorial – though plans are afoot to do this eventually where names are known – but it will tell you where your relative's unit is commemorated.

■ Another form of memorial is the Roll of Honour. This was either a book or a scroll, listing those killed in the war. Again, these were often produced by schools or firms, and were essentially a private record for colleagues and friends. The Department of Printed Books at the Imperial War Museum holds an extensive collection of them. Also, some are online, particularly at **www.roll-of-honour.com**.

Unveiling of the war memorial in Dodworth, Barnsley on 13 May 1923.

A page from the service record of Horace Sydney Dickens, providing details of the surviving members of his family. The form was completed by his widow Louisa in July 1919.

SERVICE RECORDS

The key to finding out about someone's career during the First World War is his service record. Each man's entry, progress and departure was meticulously documented so a pension could be paid to him, and hundreds of thousands of these dossiers can still be found at The National Archives at Kew.

Other ranks

Unfortunately, about 60 per cent of records for other ranks were destroyed by enemy action during the Second World War. Numerous others were salvaged and, although damaged, are partly legible. Unburnt Documents, comprising about 4,000 reels of microfilm, are in series WO 364 at Kew, while Burnt Documents are in WO 363.

For more about the records, read The National Archives's research guide *British Army Soldiers' Papers: First World War, 1914–1918* at **www.nationalarchives.gov.uk/ catalogue/ RdLeaflet.asp?sLeafletID=18**. These records can paint a detailed and fascinating picture of an individual's military experiences. You may be able to see the form signed when he reported for duty; the results of his medical examination; along with transfers; promotions; active service; wounds or illnesses; qualifications and awards gained; the time, place and reason for his demobilisation; and perhaps letters written by him or about him. These documents are now being scanned and placed online by Ancestry at **www.ancestry.co.uk/military**. They should all be available by the middle of 2009.

Records for the Household Cavalry (Life Guards and Royal Horse Guards) are in series WO 400.

You will find records for Royal Navy ratings in ADM 188, ADM 337 and ADM 116, while Royal Marine Other Ranks records up to 1925 are in ADM 157, ADM 158 and ADM 159. Records of the Royal Naval Division, a unique group of sailors who fought on land, are located in ADM 339.

For a Royal Air Force ancestor go to AIR 79.

Officers

It is usually easier to find out about officers than about other ranks. For instance, every man who received a commission is mentioned in the Army List. This has been published regularly since the middle of the 18th century, and a virtually complete set can be consulted in the microfilm reading room at Kew. During the First World War it appeared in weighty volumes every month. The Royal Navy also published a similar list, as did the Royal Air Force. By consulting these volumes it is possible to find the date on which an officer was commissioned, and to trace his career progress through subsequent editions.

The main series of officers' service records were destroyed during the Blitz; what survives is

Orders of Battle enable you to establish where a particular unit fitted into the chain of command so you can pinpoint where your relative served.

You will find these on The Long Long Trail website at **www.1914-1918.net**, and in series WO 95 at The National Archives, as well as in official campaign histories.

Once you have identified the battalion to which he belonged, the Order of Battle will tell you the brigade and the division to which it was attached. This should widen the scope of your search, because there are often histories of these formations.

War diaries are a useful source of first-hand information on the actions of a particular unit. The one below describes the action at Joncourt in September 1918.

a supplementary series. Here you will find one category for Regulars (professional, career officers) and Emergency Reserve (enlisted for the duration) officers, which are classified at Kew in WO 339. The other category, for Territorial, or Reserve, officers, is in WO 374. The easiest way to find the reference for the service record is to type a surname and initials into The National Archives's online catalogue. You can also see the original document at Kew. For more information, read The National Archives research guide *British Army Officers' Records: First World War 1914–1918*.

Naval officers' records covering the war are in ADM 340, ADM 337, ADM 273 and ADM 240. You can see Royal Marines officers' records up to 1925 in ADM 196.

RAF officers are in AIR 76.

Incidentally, one part of the Army is not included in the records at Kew – the five Foot Guards regiments of the Household Brigade. Anyone researching a relative, whether an officer or other rank, must contact the individual unit through regimental headquarters (see addresses at the end).

It is also worth noting that records of men whose military careers continued beyond 1920 are still kept by the Ministry of Defence. For contact details see the addresses section. Only next of kin can apply for these records, and there is a £30 fee.

Service records, however extensive, do not offer a complete view of a man's military career, such as any battles in which they may have fought. You will have to study the relevant war diary or regimental history to find out what a particular unit was doing during the period when your ancestor belonged to it.

WAR DIARIES

Every unit on active service kept an official record of its activities, which had to be updated each day. Often written with a stub of pencil in the darkness of a dug-out, these documents are difficult to decipher owing to their age and the untidy handwriting. Depending on their author, the entries can vary between the perfunctory – listing only essential events without going into detail – and the expansive. In the latter case, names of officers – though almost certainly not of soldiers – might be mentioned, and there may even be anecdotes. These diaries are a highly useful source of first-hand information about the realities of service at a particular time and place, and can give a vivid impression of life in a particular unit.

They are held at Kew in series WO 95, arranged according to theatre of operations, then by army, corps and division. They are slowly being made available online, and you can purchase sections of various war diaries through the Documents Online service on The National Archives's website (**www.nationalarchives. gov.uk/documentsonline**).

To illuminate these written descriptions, there is a related collection of trench maps in WO 153.

Every RAF squadron had an operational record book – the equivalent of an Army war diary. Some squadron records are with The National Archives in AIR 1, though the RAF Museum also has a good collection of pilot log books.

In the Navy, each vessel had a ship's log. However, this was almost entirely concerned with the vessel's movements and weather conditions; it is very unlikely to contain information on individual members of the crew. Ships' logs are at Kew in ADM 53.

MEDAL ROLLS

If service records for your ancestor were among those destroyed, you will at least find basic information in the Medal Index Cards at The National Archives, which list those who received campaign medals. These were intended to recognise that a soldier had been present in a theatre of war at a particular time. The awards in question were:

- **The 1914 Star** for those who saw service in Northern Europe before 22 November 1914
- **The 1914–15 Star**, for men who went overseas before the end of 1915
- **The British War Medal**
- **The Victory Medal**
- **The Territorial Force War Medal**
- **The Silver War Badge**, a lapel badge to be worn on civilian clothing

1914 STAR

1914–15 STAR

BRITISH WAR MEDAL

by men who had been honourably discharged from the services during wartime.

Each medal is engraved with the recipient's name, number and unit.

Although not complete, the Medal Index Cards are probably the most comprehensive listing of men who served in the First World War. Men not posted overseas did not qualify, and officers, where they were entitled, had to apply for their medals. If they did not, their names will not appear. You can view the cards online at **www.nationalarchives.gov.uk/ documentsonline**, **www.ancestry.co.uk/military**, or in the microfilm reading room at Kew.

Gallantry medals, the best known being the Victoria Cross, were won for an act of bravery. The National Archives holds records on everyone who received such medals, but these may not be very detailed. Lesser awards, though still highly impressive, are so comparatively numerous that

VICTORY MEDAL

TERRITORIAL FORCE WAR MEDAL

SILVER WAR BADGE

Medal Index Card

Every man and woman in the Armed services were entitled to at least two campaign medals – the Victory and British War medals. In addition, men who served overseas before 22 November 1914 received the 1914 Star (sometimes called the Mons Star) and the end of December the 1914–15 Star. In addition, men who were invalided out because of sickness or

wounds could wear the Silver War Badge.

Brief details of everyone awarded these medals were recorded on Medal Index Cards. Those for officers and ratings in the Royal Navy are series in series ADM 171 at The National Archives. Army and RAF ones are on microfiche in the Open Reading Room at Kew and available online at **www.nationalarchives.gov.uk/**

documentsonline and **www.ancestry.co.uk/military**.

They are important because they give basic details for all men, including for those whose service records have been lost.

There were several different card designs, although all contain the same information. We have chosen the most common.

Name – usually full, sometimes with a middle initial

Service number (where it exists) – useful in trying to identify your ancestor, but not given in this case because George Paterson was an officer

Medals awarded includes the roll on which the medals are recorded. The rolls are in series WO 329, but don't tell you anything which isn't on the card except battalion number (which will be useful in finding war diaries)

Unit – usually in abbreviated form. If he moved between regiments this will be shown as well

Rank, normally at time of discharge. Occasionally promotions may be shown

Gives theatre of war served in, normally "France and Belgium". The date of arrival overseas is also given

Remarks – these may include the date when the medals were dispatched, date of death or discharge, or perhaps a note that the medals had been returned because the recipient had moved

F.A.N.Y. drivers crank up their lorry.

no register can provide much personal detail.

Names of medal winners are published in the *London Gazette*, the official Government newspaper. Those relating to the two world wars can now be searched through the *London Gazette* Online Archive at **www.gazettes-online.co.uk**. There might be two mentions of a medal – notification (announcement) and citation (the reasons it was given), although citations are likely to be included only for the higher gallantry awards.

PRISONERS OF WAR

If your relative was one of the 194,000 prisoners of Germany and its allies, there is little chance you will be able to discover much about his time in captivity.

Prisoners who escaped or were repatriated were debriefed on arrival home. Reports of these interviews are in series WO 161 at Kew, although most have been lost. Scanned images of surviving records can be seen on **www.nationalarchives.gov.uk/documentsonline**.

The International Red Cross holds POW records at its headquarters in Switzerland. Contact: Archives Division and Research Service, International Committee of the Red Cross, 19 Avenue de la Paix, CH-1202 Geneva. There is a research fee.

You will find personal accounts of prisoners' experiences at the Imperial War Museum in the departments of printed books and documents and the Sound Archive.

A nurse at a casualty clearing station is presented with a dog which some wounded Canadians have brought out of the trenches, in October 1916.

WOMEN'S WORK

The contribution made by women during the conflict was immense. For the first time they joined the armed forces: 57,000 of them served with the Army alone between 1917 and 1921.

In 1917 the Women's Army Auxiliary Corps (WAAC) and Women's Royal Naval Service (WRNS) were founded, followed the next year by the Women's Royal Air Force (WRAF).

A host of nursing organisations – several well established by the outbreak of war – represented another aspect of female service. They included the First Aid Nursing Yeomanry (FANY), Voluntary Aid Detachments (VAD), Territorial Force Nursing Service, Queen Alexandra's Imperial Military Nursing Service, plus a number of others. There are published histories of many of these. Records of VADs are held either by the British Red Cross Museum and Archives, 44 Moorfields, London EC2Y 9AL, **www.redcross.org.uk**, or the Order of St John, St John's Gate, St John's Lane, London EC1M 4DA, **www.sja.org.uk**.

Surviving service records are with The National Archives. You can see WAAC papers in WO 398; Army nurses in WO 399; WRNS in ADM 318 (officers) or ADM 336 (ratings); and WRAC in AIR 80, all online at Documents Online.

You will also find useful records at the three service museums. The National Army Museum holds the archive and collections of the Women's Royal Army Corps, the successor to the WAAC. The Royal Naval Museum has similar material relating to the WRNS, while the RAF Museum covers the history of the WRAF.

Women also filled a multitude of civilian jobs as men left to enlist, working as truck drivers and bus conductresses, police officers and coal-heavers. Hundreds of thousands also took jobs in factories – much of the ammunition used by British and Allied forces was made by women.

The most important resource for any study of women in the war is the Women's Work Collection at the Imperial War Museum. It covers all aspects of military, medical, industrial and social service during and after the conflict.

USEFUL ADDRESSES

The National Archives, Ruskin Avenue, Kew, Richmond, Surrey TW9 4DU; telephone 020 8876 3444. The website, **www.nationalarchives.gov.uk**, is packed with useful information. Helpful research guides point you in the right direction, while Documents Online allows you to access material for £3.50 per record.

Commonwealth War Graves Commission, 2 Marlow Road, Maidenhead, Berkshire SL6 7DX; telephone 01628 634221; **www.cwgc.org**.

Imperial War Museum, Lambeth Road, London SE1 6HZ; telephone 020 7416 5342; **www.iwm.org.uk**. Founded in 1917 as a repository for relics of the conflict and a national memorial to those who took part in it, the IWM is an excellent place to put the experiences of those you are researching in context.

National Army Museum, Royal Hospital Road, London SW3 4HT; telephone 020 7730 0717; **www.national-army-museum.ac.uk**.

Many Army corps and regiments have their own collections, open to the public insofar as circumstances permit. Although not likely to have any records relating to individual soldiers, their archives – particularly regimental journals – may provide a windfall. The Army Museums Ogilby Trust, **www.armymuseums.org.uk**, publishes a guide, *Military Museums in the UK*, with contact details.

National Maritime Museum, Romney Road, Greenwich, London SE10 9NF; telephone 020 8858 4422; **www.nmm.ac.uk**.

Royal Naval Museum, HM Naval Base (PP66), Portsmouth PO1 3NH; telephone 023 9272 7562; **www.royalnavalmuseum.org.uk**.

Royal Air Force Museum, Graham Park Way, London NW9 5LL; telephone 020 8205 2266; **www.rafmuseum.org.uk**.

Royal Marines Museum, Eastney Barracks, Southsea, Hampshire PO4 9PX; telephone 023 9281 9385; **www.royalmarinesmuseum.co.uk**.

For Brigade of Guards other ranks, apply to: Regimental Headquarters Grenadier/Coldstream/Scots/Irish/Welsh Guards, Wellington Barracks, Birdcage Walk, London SW1E 6HQ.

For the service records of Army soldiers and officers who served after 1920 or 1922 respectively, contact: Army Personnel Centre, Disclosures 4, MP 400, Kentigern House, 65 Brown Street, Glasgow G2 8EX; **www.veterans-uk.info**.

For the Service Records of Royal Naval personnel from 1924, apply to: Data Protection Cell, Director Naval Career Management, Disclosure Cell, Room 109, Victory Building, HM Naval Base, Portsmouth, PO1 3LS.

For the service records of Royal Air Force Personnel from 1920, apply to: RAF Disclosure of Information Office, PMA 1B (RAF), Room 5, Building 248A, RAF Personnel Management Agency, RAF Innsworth, Gloucester GL3 1EZ.

The Western Front Association website at **www.westernfront.co.uk** is dedicated to the study the war in France and Flanders. There are other associations for different campaigns, but this is the largest and most well known.

MEDALS
and the family historian

You may well possess medals that were once awarded to a ancestor. **John Sly** explains how these small survivors of history can help you to find out more about your forebears

Medals, for those who know little or nothing about them can be frustrating as well as fascinating. They can be an informative source of information as well as being a splendid link with our ancestors.

British campaign, gallantry, and long service medals provide five main elements of information that will help family historians:

■ Identification of the medal(s) fixes the historical context.

■ The clasps on the medals focuses the context and provides key dating information.

■ (In the case of groups of medals) the whole group indicates the span of a military career in terms of campaigns in which the serviceman took part.

■ Long service medals indicate service of at least 18 years for the Army or 15 years for the Royal Navy or Royal Marines (the number of years for qualifying changed over the course of time, but these figures can be regarded as the minimum period).

■ The naming details give an indication of the status of the individual to whom the medal was awarded at the time the medal was issued.

Taking these elements in order, the first thing to do is to identify the medal(s). Faced with these unfamiliar objects, which are almost always small works of art in their own right, many family historians may well be daunted as to what to do, but usually the medals come with the ribbons with which they were originally issued, and each ribbon is uniquely coloured.

Let us look at what are probably the three most common British medals in existence today, and which most family historians will have come across even if they have not physically handled them: the medals which

Deborah Pownall

were issued for service during the First World War – that is the 1914 (or 1914–15) Star, the British War Medal, and the Allied Victory Medal.

Millions of British ex-servicemen wore these medals in the early 1920s when they were issued in huge numbers, and there are thousands of photographs showing men (usually men, but there were many women who were also entitled to these medals in their own right) wearing these objects on the left breast. For identification purposes, the ribbons are respectively described as watered silk red merging into white merging into blue; orange watered centre with stripes of white and black at each side and borders of royal blue; and double rainbow, indigo at edges and red in centre.

So, having found a group like this, which can be described thus, the family historian wants to set about identifying them. How can this be done easily? Although there are many books on medals available in public libraries, the best is *Medal Year Book*, which contains descriptions and illustrations of all British (and many foreign) medals, military and civilian. There are various websites which contain illustrations of medals, but none are comprehensive or particularly easy to use.

Clasps

Having identified the medal, and having read something about it, the reader will now discover whether or not there are clasps issued with it. A clasp (sometimes referred to as a 'bar') is usually a small oblong-shaped piece of metal (normally silver) attached to the medal, generally speaking by rivets, identifying specific service in relation to the medal. As there were no clasps awarded for the Great War medals discussed above, I will offer you, as an example, two more relatively common medals that were issued with clasps: the

medals for the Boer War – known respectively as the Queen's and King's South Africa Medals.

The reason for the two medals was that Queen Victoria, in whose name the war had been declared in 1899, died before the war was concluded on 31 May 1902, and the new king, Edward VII, wanted to issue a medal in his own name to recognise service after the death of his mother. These two medals very neatly sum up what can be so helpful, but also so confusing about medals.

The clasps (there were 26 of them in all) for the Queen's Medal were issued according to strict rules. They can be divided into three types, which for convenience we can call: state, date and battle. The first two are almost self-explanatory: an example of a state clasp is Cape Colony. A medal bearing this clasp denotes that active service had been performed in the Cape Colony between 11 October 1899 and 31 May 1902, but that the recipient had not been present at a battle in the colony that was otherwise commemorated by a clasp. A date clasp, such as South Africa 1901, denoted that the recipient had seen active service during the year 1901, but had not qualified for the King's Medal, which required at least 18 months service in South Africa before the serviceman could be eligible. A battle clasp, like Paardeberg, was issued to "all troops within 7,000 yards of General Cronje's final laager between midnight of 17 February and midnight of 26 February 1900, and to all troops within 7,000 yards of Koodoe's Rand Drift between those dates." As Paardeberg was in the Orange Free State, the recipient could not therefore receive the Orange Free State clasp. So, a medal that combined these two clasps would have to be wrong.

All the medal rolls for the Boer War can be

1. **Distinguished Service Order (DSO)**, in this instance a double gallantry award, the second award being indicated by the bar on the ribbon.
2. The 1914–15 Star.
3. The British War Medal.
4. The Allied Victory Medal. The oak leaf signifies that the holder had been mentioned in despatches.
5. Second World War defence medal.
6. The Coronation medal.
7. Légion d'Honneur. (Awarded for working with French forces).

found in series WO 100 at
The National Archives at Kew.

Gallantry medals

Gallantry medals are often a
boon to the family historian,
because it makes an individual
serviceman, particularly other
ranks, stand out from the
crowd. Officers are usually well
documented, but information
about Other Ranks is much more elusive. A
gallantry award makes the ordinary
serviceman more prominent, and they will
almost certainly have been mentioned in the
national or local press, or in a regimental
journal. All gallantry awards were listed in the
London Gazette and this can further research.

For the period of the First World War there
are citations available (almost always in the
case of single acts of bravery) for the Victoria
Cross, Distinguished Service Order, Military
Cross, Distinguished Conduct Medal,
Conspicuous Gallantry Medal, Distinguished
Service Cross, and Distinguished Flying Cross.
These specify the act for which the medal was
awarded, and although the date of the action is
rarely included, the date of the award at least
gives an approximate date when it was earned.

Further research can then be undertaken in
war diaries, ships' logs or squadron records as
appropriate. For the Second World War,
citations for Army gallantry medals can
be found in WO 373 and online at The
National Archives's Documents Online
service.

Some gallantry medals, especially
those with enamel decoration, were
issued un-named. So, the discovery of,
for example, a medal of the
Distinguished Service Order, on its
own, would not identify the recipient
unless it were accompanied by a
certificate of some kind.

Long service medals

Long service and good conduct
medals, which are issued to members
of the regular forces or of the
territorial or volunteer forces, may also
be researched, and dates of award can
be established. It is then possible to derive an
estimate of the date of enlistment for the
recipient. The existence of an Army long
service medal in the 19th century almost
always indicates that the soldier was
discharged to pension, which means that the

The Queen's (above)
and King's (below)
South Africa Medals
showing clasps
awarded for taking part
in particular actions.

Capt. Richard Leonard Atkinson, R.W.
Surr. R.
For conspicuous gallantry and initiative.
When his Company Commander was killed
he at once assumed command, reorganised
the company and, with great bravery, led it
to its final objective, which he successfully
consolidated.

The citation in the *London Gazette* for 18 July 1917
recording the action of Captain Richard Atkinson in
the First World War for which he was awarded the
Military Cross.

chances of finding a service record in the
WO 97 series are very much higher than they
otherwise might be. Medal rolls are in series
WO 101 and WO 102 for the Army, and
ADM 171 for the Royal Navy.

Names and numbers

Perhaps the most important information on a
British medal is the name. For medals issued
before about 1860, neither the Army nor the
Royal Navy saw fit to include numbers with the
name, even though individual numbers had
been used regularly since about 1830 by the
Army and 1853 by the Royal Navy and
Royal Marines.

After 1860, regimental (and after 1920
Army) numbers were always included for all
ranks other than officers (who
were not numbered in the same
way as Other Ranks). A similar
format was used by the
Royal Navy, and later by the
Royal Air Force.
Naming details include four
elements that can be very useful
for the family historian:
■ number (where included);
■ rank or rate:
■ name (usually initials and
surname);
■ unit.
Taken together, these details
identify a unique individual,
but the separate elements can
tell a story in their own right.
For Other Ranks, the number
is a key element of a
serviceman's personal details. It is unique to
the individual.

In the Royal Navy and Royal Marines after
1853, service numbers were allocated mainly
chronologically, that is without any relationship
at all to the ship in which a man served. This

Reverse of the War Service
Medal issued after the
Second World War to all
British and Commonwealth
military personnel.

was because sailors and marines changed ships on a regular basis, and because ships also allocated local numbers to individuals as they signed on, thus the service number was issued centrally, and was retained by the serviceman throughout his naval career.

In the Army, up to 1920, the number was allocated by the regiment. This is very important, as it means that a soldier who changed regiment also changed number. It is therefore possible to find a group of, say, four medals to the same man, showing different numbers and regiments, but only detailed research in regimental musters (in series WO 12 at Kew), which record all such transfers and movements, will confirm that this is the same man. For the First World War the military index cards often give the various regimental numbers assigned to an individual.

After 1920 an Army number was issued when a man enlisted, and this number was retained throughout his service career, regardless of which regiment or corps he was serving with.

With medals, where naming mistakes are legion (usually wrong initial/s, or the wrong spelling of a name), the number is crucial as a means of unique identification and of distinguishing one man from another.

Misspellings could be repeated ad infinitum until they appeared on a medal roll. Incorrect initials are common, particularly on the Queen's and King's South Africa medals, for some reason. However, there is usually another way to confirm the correct details from other contemporary documents, and medals that may appear to be bogus can turn out to be perfectly genuine.

The appearance of the rank on a medal can be helpful, but it can also be misleading. During the Great War, soldiers were regularly promoted from the ranks. The naming rules that applied for medals were as follows:

■ for the 1914 and 1914–15 Star, the rank stamped on the medal was the rank held at the time of the recipient first entering a theatre of war;

■ for the British War and Victory Medals, the rank was the highest rank achieved (substantive, temporary or acting) overseas.

This means that there are many sets of medals in existence issued to Army personnel where the 1914–15 Star records a man as a Private, with a number and a regiment, while the British War and Victory medals may record him as, for example, Captain, but with

Medal terms and definitions

Bar	The second and subsequent awards of gallantry medals. So called because a clasp or bar was placed on the ribbon marking the award.
Campaign medal	Issued for participation in a particular campaign.
Citation	A brief description of the reasons for the award of a gallantry medal. Those for the Victoria and George crosses and a few other gallantry medals were published in the London Gazette, but generally they can be found in papers and files relating to medal awards.
Clasp	Awarded for service in action at particular battles or actions. It is a metal bar fitted on the ribbon of the relevant campaign medal.
Decorations	Tend to be used to recognise specific deeds of heroism. They include the Victoria and George crosses, the Military Cross and Military Medal.
Gallantry Medals	Issued for acts of bravery, such as taking an enemy position under fire or rescuing wounded comrades.
Gazetted	The date that notification of an award has been published in the London Gazette.
General Service Medal	Issued to cover a number of smaller actions or campaigns for which no seperate campaign medal was issued. The action would be noted in a clasp.
Group	Two or more medals normally worn in a row. On the left will be any gallantry medals, in the centre – campaign medals, and to the right (as you look at it) – long service, conduct and foreign awards.
London Gazette	The official newspaper published by the British government. Details of all gallantry medals are listed here.
Medal Index Card	Technically an index to the medal rolls of campaign medals issued during the First World War. They contain details of individual servicemen.
Medal roll	The list of names of persons awarded a campaign or gallantry medal. Some have been reprinted by specialist publishers.
Medals	Are used to recognise bravery, long and valuable service or good conduct.
Mentions in Despatches	The lowest form of gallantry award. No medal is issued, although the recipients are listed in the London Gazette. After 1920 recipients could wear an oak leaf on the appropriate campaign medal ribbon on their uniform.
Miniature	A smaller copy of the full size award worn on dinner jackets or mess kits as opposed to the full sized ones that are normally only worn on a uniform.
Naming	The policy of placing individuals' names on the rim, or reverse, of campaign medals.
Obverse	The front of the medal, normally with the sovereign's portrait on.
Order	An order is perhaps the most elaborate form of medals, typically awarded for distinguished services to a nation. An order differs from other forms of medal in that it often implies a membership of an organisation, such as the Order of the Garter or Companion of Honour.
Reverse	The back of the medal generally with the design unique to the type of medal.
Ribbon	Has a unique design often reflecting the services involved in the campaign or the place where the medal was awarded.
Ribbon bar	Ribbons worn on uniform when the medals themselves are not worn; medals themselves are usually only worn at official parades.
Rim	The side of a medal often inscribed with the name of the holder, his unit and service number.
Watered	A feature on ribbons where colours appear to fade into each other.

Second World War Campaign medals

Every serviceman and woman who met certain criteria (normally being present for 90 days in a particular theatre of operations) could claim up to five campaign medals.

As a general rule, most service personnel were not issued with medals before they were demobilised. Consequently they had to claim them after they had left the services. Only those men and women who remained in the Armed Forces received their medals automatically. Although the availability of medals for wartime service was widely advertised at the time, many people did not claim them.

Even now, over 60 years later, several hundred veterans or their next of kin make an initial claim for Second World War medals every month. They are still issued in the first instance free of charge. Medals can be issued to the legal next of kin of deceased service personnel, but proof of kinship is required.

To claim medals, replace stolen or destroyed medals, or find out whether an individual is entitled, please write to the MoD Medal Office (address opposite). You will need to supply service number, unit (Army and Marines), and branch or trade (RAF and RN), full name, date of birth, rank and date of discharge.

As large numbers of people are claiming their medals, there is usually a backlog. Claims are dealt with as quickly as possible. Every effort is made to acknowledge and process claims in a timely manner, but checking and verification is a time-consuming process. For more information visit **www.veterans-uk.info**.

MOD Medal Office
Building 250
RAF Innsworth
Gloucester GL3 1HW
Telephone 0800 058 3600
www.veterans-uk.info/medals/medals.html

Eight separate campaign medals were issued, although no more than five could be worn by an individual. As a cost-saving measure medals were not inscribed with the names of the individuals to whom they were awarded, although a number of individuals subsequently had inscriptions added privately.

MEDAL	RIBBON	NOTES
1939–1945 Star	Three equal stripes of dark blue, scarlet and light blue representing the three armed services.	This was the basic war service star and was generally awarded to men who had completed six months' active service (two months for aircrew) overseas. It was the only medal awarded to men who saw service in France and Norway in 1940, and Greece and Crete in 1941. Those awarded this star were eligible for others if they served in other theatres of operation.
Air Crew Europe Star	A broad central light blue stripe, black borders and narrow yellow stripes, for the sky, the night and searchlight beams.	Awarded to RAF crews for operational flights over Europe.
Atlantic Star	Three shaded equal stripes of dark blue, white and green.	Generally awarded to the Royal and Merchant Navy who served in convoys across the North Atlantic, but members of the RAF and Army attached to the RN and Merchant Navy also received it.
Africa Star	Pale buff with a broad central scarlet stripe and two narrow stripes of dark blue (to the left) and mid blue (to the right).	Awarded for one or more day's service anywhere in North Africa before 12 May 1943.
Burma Star	A central red stripe and two narrower blue and yellow stripes on either side.	Awarded for service in India and Burma.
Italy Star	Equal stripes of red, white, green, white and red representing the Italian flag.	Awarded for service in Italy, the Balkans and southern France between 11 June 1943 and 8 May 1945.
Pacific Star	Dark green with scarlet edges, a central yellow stripe, a narrow dark blue stripe on the left side and a light blue one to the right.	Also awarded to personnel who served in Hong Kong and Malaya.
Defence Medal	Green (for the fields of Britain), with a wide central orange stripe (the flames of the Blitz) and two narrow black stripes either side (for those who lost their lives during the bombing).	Awarded to all those who served in a military capacity in Britain, Malta and British colonies between September 1939 and May 1945, including civilians and members of the Home Guard.
War Service Medal	The colours of the Union Flag going from red to blue to white from each edge and a narrow central red stripe.	Issued to anyone who had 28 days service in uniform or with an accredited organisation.

Reverse of (left) the
Mercantile Marine War
Medal, and (right)
British War Medal.

no number and no regiment. Only reference to the Medal Index Cards at Kew (also available online) will establish whether the combination is either possible or likely, and this indicates how important it is to have all the relevant information, particularly if your ancestor had a common name.

The unit of which a serviceman was a member is the last item with the name. Army medals invariably record the regiment or corps (there are a few exceptions, the most obvious of which is officers' medals from the First World War), Royal Navy medals record the ship in which the sailor or marine served, but Royal Air Force medals rarely record the squadron, contenting themselves with the designation RAF.

Finding a medal (or medals) that record a soldier's name, rank, number and unit is therefore a wonderful start to research. Complications, however, can arise when men changed units, but the medals they received did not reflect this.

Not all British campaign medals are stamped with individual names. The first large group chronologically are the medals for the Crimean War. Although these are usually found named, they were originally issued un-named, but could be returned to the Mint by the recipient for naming.

More recent are the campaign medals and stars of the Second World War. For whatever reason – expense is the reason usually quoted – the post-war government decided not to stamp these medals with the recipients names, and it is quite possible to find groups of medals including a Distinguished Service Order and a Distinguished Flying Cross with not one named medal in the group.

Civilian medals

Medals, of course, have been awarded to civilians as well as to armed service personnel, including the Police, Firemen, medical and other emergency services, as well as ordinary citizens.

It is important to note that medals that were awarded to the armed services were also awarded to civilians. The names of civilians appear on many campaign medals, and these can be some of the most fruitful for family historians.

Civilians were also awarded gallantry medals such as the George Cross and George Medal, the Albert Medal and the two Edward Medals (Mines and Industry respectively). Thus many of the stories behind these awards are full of local historical detail, and can open up new trails for family historians to follow.

The background to the awards of police

medals for gallantry (such as the King's/Queen's Police Medal), as well as lists of other medals like the County and Borough police medals, can be found in Home Office files at Kew. There are also long service medals, jubilee and coronation medals awarded to a variety of civilian employees who were involved in the respective ceremonies in some way. Any junior civil servant who served long enough and was of excellent character could also be awarded the Imperial Service Order (later the Imperial Service Medal).

TAKING IT FURTHER

For those who know little or nothing about medals, I recommend starting with *Medal Year Book* (Token Publishing, new edition published annually). This is the only complete guide between one set of covers to all British (and many foreign) campaign, gallantry and long service medals. Another invaluable introduction is William Spencer's *Medals: a researcher's guide* (The National Archives, 2006). In addition, Peter Duckers has written a series of excellent and handsomely illustrated booklets for Shire Publications on gallantry and campaign medals.

There are also many published medal rolls and compilations of award holders. The National Archives's library has many of these titles, and some can be found in large reference libraries as well.

The *London Gazette* is the method by which various official data has been published relating to government and the Crown since the 1660s. This includes information relating to the commissioning, promotion and resignation or retirement of officers in the services, as well as providing lists of all those who have been honoured or decorated by the sovereign. This includes details of all gallantry medals as well as foreign decorations (although the records for foreign awards are not comprehensive). It is available online, in a fully searchable form, at **www.gazettes-online.co.uk**.

Army Orders (sometimes called General Orders) are published regularly by the Army, and as well as recording information relating to uniforms, discipline, training and other routine issues for managing the Army, they also included, up to 1916, lists of awards of long service medals. After 1916 the lists of names no longer appeared in the published Army Orders but were confined to a supplement issued with the Orders. A set can be found in series WO 123 at Kew. RAF long service medal holders between 1918 and 1936 are found in the Air Ministry Orders in AIR 72.

Local regimental museums can often help researchers (if they have the resources) because regimental journals frequently contain biographical material that is impossible to find elsewhere. The best approach is to write a letter, setting out exactly what you would like to know, and including a stamped addressed envelope for a reply. A list with links can be found at **www.armymuseums.org.uk**.

A very good source of information about medals and associated subjects is the library of the National Army Museum. In order to use this facility you will need a readers ticket. These cannot be issued on the day, so you will need to telephone in advance for an application form.

The National Archives have published several online research guides, although almost all medal rolls can be found in WO 100 for the Army and ADM 171 for the Royal Navy (there are as yet no medal rolls for the Royal Air Force). Medal rolls, however, can turn up in the most unlikely and obscure places. They are listed in full in William Spencer's book.

GOING BACK
BEFORE 1837

Parish registers are some of the oldest records, and in many places have been kept for over four centuries. But if you don't where your ancestors lived, try an index. **Anthony Adolph** shows where to find the best examples

When you start to trace your ancestors back into the early-nineteenth century, you'll increasingly have to rely on parish registers. In some ways this is good because there are several nationwide indexes. However, the records were often poorly kept or just do not survive which can make using them very frustrating.

The Anglican, or Church of England, was by law the established church. Until 1837 it was compulsory for you to baptise your children, get married and be buried by the church. The Church was also responsible for proving wills (see page 20) and had a role in running secular affairs in rural parishes.

There were (and indeed still are) some 16,000 parishes across England and Wales – most villages were within a single parish, although towns had two or more parishes depending on their size and the wealth of local benefactors in medieval times. As well as the incumbent vicar or rector, each parish elected two churchwardens, and in larger or wealthier districts appointed a clerk who was responsible for maintaining the registers and keeping safe parish records.

If the clergy and their clerks were conscientious then that is a great bonus for family historians. However this was not always the case. In Richmond, Surrey the same family held the post of clerk who, according to the transcriber of the records, "passed on from each generation to the next, a tradition of slovenliness and neglect in regard to their duty." This means of course that many baptisms, marriages and deaths were either not recorded or incompletely noted in the register and are thus lost for good.

Although the Church of England was the only legal church, that it does not mean that there were not other churches engaged in worship. Roman Catholics, for example, did not entirely disappear with the Reformation in the 17th century. Despite terrible persecution, parts of south Lancashire remained loyal to the old religion, as did odd pockets elsewhere, especially where a local landowning family remained believers. A bigger threat to the Church however, came from newer denominations. These Nonconformists, as they were known, began with the Quakers and Baptists in the mid-17th century. The most important sect however was the Methodists, who came to prominence during the 18th century. All this means that you may need to check the records of these other faiths as well as the Anglican parish registers to find your ancestors. See the next section for an article about them.

Parish registers were first kept in 1538. Few records, however, survive before the beginning of the 17th century. The only major change since then was the introduction of printed forms in 1813 in which specified details on baptism and burials are entered.

The survival of early registers is patchy, and they can be depressingly unhelpful. Baptismal entries are often little more than the child's name, who the father was, and when the event took place.

Baptisms normally occurred within a few days of the birth. If the child was born out of wedlock this would also be noted, and the mother's name given. Before 1754, entries for weddings usually contain the names of the spouses, with perhaps a note if one of them was born outside the parish. After 1754 however, marriage entries had to be entered in special registers and are a little more informative.

Death registers normally just contain the name of the deceased, although occasionally their age and occupation is noted.

Matters are made worse by the relatively few Christian names in general use. You may well find three or four babies with the same forename and surname christened within a

Banns or licences

When people married, they had to promise that they were legally entitled to do so – that they were old enough, not very closely related, and not about to commit bigamy. Banns and licenses further ensured that this was the case.

Banns were read out in church on three successive Sundays before the wedding. The banns readings gave the rest of the congregation the opportunity to expose liars or bigamists. Banns were sometimes recorded in a banns book which, where they survive, can be found at local record offices. If either bride or groom came from outside the parish where the marriage was due to take place, banns would be read in both parishes. The banns book for one will tell you where the other lived, which can be very handy.

If you wanted to avoid such public scrutiny, you could apply for a license from the local bishop or archdeacon. In doing so you had to swear you were entitled to marry and undertake to forfeit a bond of money if you were found out to be fibbing. Licenses were also used by people wanting to marry very quickly. They became a status symbol, used by the upper and middle classes, or those who aspired to be so.

Jeremy Gibson's *Bishops' transcripts and marriage licenses, bonds and allegations; a guide to their location and indexes*, (FFHS, 4th edn, 1997) will tell you where the licenses are to be found. Or you can ask at the record office holding the records for the relevant diocese. The Society of Genealogists also has many indexes and transcripts.

Some licenses were also issued by the Archbishops of York and Canterbury and are kept at the Borthwick Institute and Lambeth Palace Library respectively. The latter's records are partially indexed at **www.englishorigins.net**.

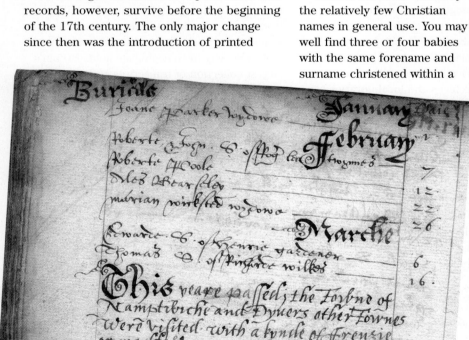

An extract listing burials from St Mary's Nantwich's register from 1586/7, with a note added by the rector referring to the high mortality to be found in the area at the time. Many parish registers have annotations relating to extraordinary events, or entries of baptisms, marriages or burials that were considered out of the ordinary.

An extract from St Mary's Nantwich burial register for 1588 and 1589, which not only lists burials, but also includes an entry about the defeat of the Spanish Armada.

St Mary's Nantwich was founded in the 14th century and has registers going back to when parishes were first ordered to keep records in 1538. This 19th century lithograph is by G Hawkins.

few months of each other, making it impossible to work out from whom you are descended.

If the register you are looking for is missing, it is worth seeing whether a duplicate – or bishop's transcript, survives. Clerks had to make regular copies and send it to the bishop for safekeeping. However, as they were not paid for this task, the quality of the transcript is often poor.

Most parish registers and bishop's transcripts are usually at local record offices, with an incomplete nationwide collection at the Society of Genealogists. It is now rare for individual churches to keep their old registers. Cecil Humphrey-Smith's *The Phillimore Atlas and Index to Parish Registers* (2nd ed, Phillimore, 1995) will tell you where registers are held. Most archives and local libraries have copies of the Atlas.

INDEXES

For all their value, parish registers can be difficult to use, either because the information was not recorded in the first place, or people moved so family events were recorded in other parishes. And, of course, men often took brides from further afield, with the wedding usually taking place in the bride's parish church.

Perhaps the greatest problem is finding an event – especially marriages. In the half-century or so before the introduction of Hardwick's Marriage Act in 1754, which outlawed the practice of clandestine marriages, there were hundreds of thousands of such weddings.

The centre for this was the area around Fleet Prison in London, where some 200,000 marriages took place between about 1710 and 1754. In the 1740s around half the marriages in London were performed here – 6,500 ceremonies a year. Registers to Fleet marriages are in series RG 7 at The National Archives and are available on microfilm. There are also some indexes online at **www. thegenealogist.co.uk**.

Using indexes to parish registers can often help you track elusive ancestors, but you should be aware they may contain errors or mistranscriptions. Entries should appear as they were spelled at the time, so if you can't find a name, try variations. If, for example, William Britton was recorded as William Britain, he won't appear in the index under Britton.

The Society of Genealogists holds Britain's largest collection of transcripts and indexes to parish registers. You can find out what they have from their website: **www.sog.org.uk**.

There are a number of indexes to the people who appear in parish registers, but none can rival the International Genealogical Index (IGI). The IGI is available on microfiche at Latter-day Saints (LDS) Church family history centres and many archives, along with libraries, including The National Archives and the Society of Genealogists. However it is most easily searched online, at **www.familysearch.org**.

Part of a register of burials at St Nicholas, Durham in 1597 noting the beginning of the Great Visitation – the plague.

It contains some 58 million English and Welsh baptism and marriage records, as well as entries for Scotland and Ireland. However, there are few burial records. Some counties, such as Kent, are very poorly covered indeed, while others, such as County Durham, are almost complete.

Furthermore, not all the registers covered are fully indexed. In some cases the marriages, but not the baptisms, of a parish may be included, or just the registers for a few years. Entries were not always taken from original records but were based on bishop's transcripts or transcripts of registers.

It is difficult to work out precisely what has been indexed, although you may get an idea from looking at the Family History Library catalogue available at **www.familysearch.org**.

In addition, the IGI does not include all the details given in original entries. On the other hand, it does include information from other sources, such as family bibles or even family stories – although these may well be inaccurate. For all these reasons, you must always, without fail, check the source of the entry and then look at the original for yourself.

More about the IGI and the pitfalls in using it can be found at **www.genuki.org.uk/big/eng/LIN/igi.html**.

The IGI is supplemented by two other indexes.

The British Isles Vital Record Index (BIVRI) has extracts from many additional parishes. The second edition was published in 2002. Material on the BIVRI is not available online, but can be seen at Kew, LDS Church family history centres and family history society research libraries. It can also be purchased from the Church for £22.95. There is a list of what it contains, arranged by county, at **www.genoot.com/downloads/BVRI2**.

The Federation of Family History Societies has published the National Burial Index (NBI). Now in its second edition, it contains some 13 million burials in Anglican church grounds for almost every county in England and Wales; it also includes some records from civic cemeteries. As with the IGI, coverage varies considerably between counties, and it is the most comprehensive for the period after 1800 between 1813 and 1837. Work on a new edition is under way.

Local studies libraries and family history society research libraries may have copies on disc. But most people access it online at **www.findmypast.com** for a fee. This website also has details of an increasing number of marriages and baptisms.

In addition, there are some specialist marriage indexes:

Boyd's Marriage Index contains about 15 per cent of marriage registers for England, and some licenses and banns books. It covers the period 1538—1837 and is especially strong on the London area. A major pitfall is that the surnames were sometimes rewritten to fit its compiler's unique phonetic system. It is available at the Society of Genealogists, and some record offices on fiche and online (for a fee) at **www.englishorigins.net www.britishorigins.net**. The database also includes Boyd's London Burials and some marriage licence indexes.

Pallot's Marriage Index covers registers from all over the country, but again is largely focused on London. It covers the period 1780–1837 and includes some registers that were destroyed in the Blitz. It is available (for a fee) on **www.ancestry.co.uk**. The original index is held by the Institute of Heraldic and Genealogical Studies in Canterbury.

The whereabouts of many smaller marriage indexes, and indexes to marriage licences around the country are given in Jeremy Gibson and Elizabeth Hampson's *Marriage and Census Indexes for Family Historians* (5th ed, FFHS, 2000). Baptism and burial indexes are covered in the authors' *Specialist Indexes for Family Historians* (2nd ed, FFHS, 2000).

A number of transcripts from parish registers and indexes, can be found online, either on sites devoted to individual parishes or villages, or at **http://freereg.rootsweb.com**.

A page from a published transcript of the baptismal register for Richmond, Surrey for 1679 and 1680.

USEFUL ADDRESSES

Borthwick Institute for Archives, University of York, Heslington, York YO10 5DD; telephone 01904 321166; **www.york.ac.uk/inst/bihr**

Institute of Heraldic and Genealogical Studies, 79–82 Northgate, Canterbury CT1 1BA; telephone 01227 768664; **www.ihgs.ac.uk**

Lambeth Palace Library, Lambeth Palace Road, London SE1 7JU; telephone 020 7898 1400; **www.lambethpalacelibrary.org**

Society of Genealogists, 14 Charterhouse Buildings, Goswell Road, London EC1M 7BA; telephone 020 7251 8799; **www.sog.org.uk**

NONCONFORMIST RECORDS

Through the centuries, different denominations – even different religions – have waxed and waned in popularity, often influenced by historical events. **Michael Gandy** explains why it is important to understand what shaped our ancestors' choices and beliefs

A Wesleyan Chapel built in 1896. The statue over the door is of John Wesley preaching.

Patterns of religious practice in Britain may have varied from century to century, but beliefs are much harder to quantify. For family historians, the historical context determines not only what the prevailing orthodoxy during a particular period was, but also what records remain for us to explore.

Since the 16th century the majority of English people have been part of the Church of England (the Anglican Church) and we find their baptisms, marriages and burials in the parish registers (see page 64).

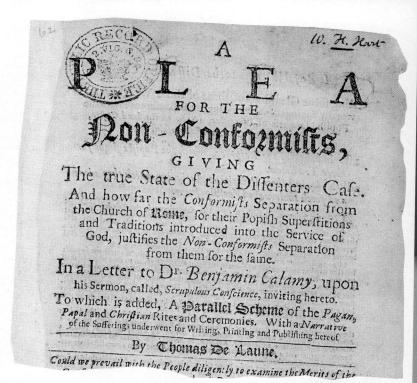

A
PLEA
FOR THE
Non-Conformists,
GIVING
The true State of the Dissenters Case,
And how far the Conformists Separation from
the Church of Rome, for their Popish Superstitions
and Traditions introduced into the Service of
God, justifies the Non-Conformists Separation
from them for the same.
In a Letter to Dr Benjamin Calamy, upon
his Sermon, called, Scrupulous Conscience, inviting hereto.
To which is added, A Parallel Scheme of the Pagan,
Papal and Christian Rites and Ceremonies. With a Narrative
of the Sufferings undergone for Writing, Printing and Publishing hereof.
By Thomas De Laune.

Dissenting tracts were widely disseminated to promote the cause of Nonconformity and religious freedom.

Yet although the Church of England rejected a lot of the old Roman Catholic beliefs and practices, many people thought it had not gone far enough.

They disliked the settlement of 1559 and the policy of Elizabeth I, who tried to found a national church that would include everyone by being flexible. These objectors were known as **Puritans** (because they thought the church needed to be purified further). By the early 17th century, they had become a very articulate, influential and conspicuous group. However, they had decided to try and change the Church of England by staying within it. so they almost all attended its services (many of them indeed were ministers), and went through the standard forms of baptism, marriage and burial, of which they did not really approve.

Thus for family historians there are no separate **Nonconformist** church records in the 16th and early 17th centuries. Sometimes we find Puritans presented before the ecclesiastical courts for expressing their opinions, but they only really came under this sort of pressure in Charles I's reign (1625–49), after William Laud became Archbishop of Canterbury in 1633.

Then came the Civil War and the Commonwealth (1642–60), when the Anglican Church lost its power (temporarily) and the Puritans were free to do what they wanted – either inside or outside their parish churches. There were three main groups:

■ Presbyterians believed in the authority of ministers, but not in the concept of bishops. They modelled themselves on the forms of the Scottish church founded by John Knox. These included very strict rules about behaviour, but in England they were never powerful enough to impose such views on everybody.

■ Congregationalists, also known as Independents and Separatists, believed in the "priesthood of all believers", whereby all godly men (and to some extent women) were equal. They came together to hear the Bible read and explained and they invited respected ministers to lead them, but fundamentally they employed the minister. If they did not like his approach, they could dismiss him.

Handy Hints

Looking for clues

Indications that you should investigate the Nonconformist registers, along with the large amounts of biographical material kept by some denominations might be:

■ a long family history of Nonconformity.

■ a number of Old Testament forenames in the family – Elijah, Hezekiah, Rebecca and so on.

■ if a post-1837 marriage took place in a Nonconformist chapel or in a register office.

■ if a parish register has a suspiciously high number of marriages and burials of one surname, in proportion to the number of baptisms.

■ The distinguishing feature of Baptists was their refusal to baptise children. Instead, they practised adult "believers' baptism". For family historians this makes them the most difficult group to trace.

Other groups which arose during the same period included: **Ranters**, **Levellers**, **Seekers**, and **Fifth Monarchy Men**. They were very religious and there is a lot of material on individuals, but they did not keep records about their families. None of these groups lasted beyond 1660, and most had no interest in formal church structures.

The **Muggletonians**, however, did survive. They were always very few in number, but the last member only died in 1979. Their records are now in the British Library.

The only group to survive this period in large numbers were the **Quakers**, whose numbers exploded dramatically in the 1650s. Quakers did not believe in any church structures – or any ministers – at all. Their belief in equality without leaders led them to develop a structure of committees with secretaries recording decisions (arrived at by consensus – Quakers would never vote) and a central headquarters in London. Lots of their records have been handed down and we can often say with confidence what Quakers thought or did.

In fact, the other groups often thought and did very much the same – and may have

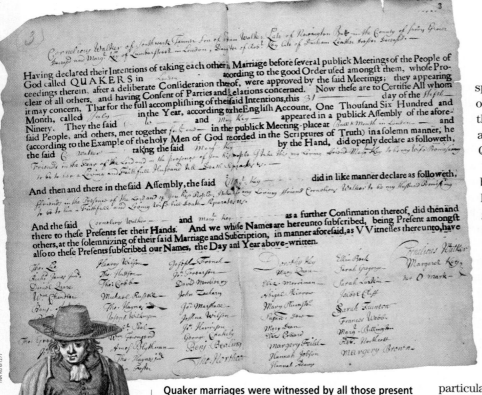

Quaker marriages were witnessed by all those present at the monthly meeting where the ceremony was performed and recorded on printed forms.

kept records of it at the time – but each meeting was independent and for the most part their records have not survived.

After the restoration of the monarchy in 1660, an Anglican parliament required the clergy to use the Book of Common Prayer without alteration, and to accept the principle of ordination. This prompted many worshippers to leave the Church of England, and for the next 30 years there was a lot of pressure on them to conform. A great many were presented at Quarter Sessions for their refusal to attend church, and those lists of names are our only systematic source for identifying such ordinary people.

However, these lists have to be used with care. Firstly, some magistrates or ministers were keener than others to punish those who were breaking the law. Secondly, the authorities often did not enquire about what

SEARCHING

Nonconformist records at The National Archives

At The National Archives you can access serveral thousand Nonconformist registers and certificates from England and Wales.

The main churches represented are the Society of Friends (or Quakers), the Presbyterians, the Independents (or Congregationalists), the Baptists, the Weslyans and other Methodists, the Moravians, the Countess of Huntingdon's Connexion, the Bible Christians, and the Swedenborgians, as well as various foreign churches.

These records are available on microfilm in the Open Reading Room at The National Archives. However, they have also been fully indexed and the indexes are available online at **www.familysearch.org** or in the International Genealogical Index (IGI). The IGI is available at the Society of Genealogists, or at the LDS Church (Mormon) family history centres around the country.

Digital images of the Nonconformist registers are also available at **www.thegenealogist.co.uk** for a fee.

specific reasons they had for not obeying the law, with the result that all the various groups are mixed together and the same list may contain Baptists, Quakers and Catholics.

All the main denominations have been thoroughly researched, often by local historians or people interested in general theological or political trends, rather than individuals or families. Even if you are confident you know to which type of Nonconformity your ancestors belonged, it is always worth searching publications about all groups. Your Baptist ancestors may be in a list published by a Catholic or Quaker society – and vice versa.

Family historians naturally think in terms of families sticking to a particular denomination, but both individuals and groups may chop and change. My family in Great Budworth, Cheshire, were Puritan Anglicans until the Civil War, then they were Baptists. In 1654 my ancestors, William and Edward Gandy, converted to Quakerism, while their uncle, Hugh Gandy, and his children stayed Baptist. Other relatives remained Anglican.

Noncomformists achieved a legal assurance of toleration through the Act of Settlement in 1689, and in 1691 they were granted permission to meet, and construct separate buildings if they wanted, provided they registered their meeting places at Quarter Sessions. From this time on we begin to get registers of baptism (though very few go back this far). However, a comparison of the known baptism registers (almost all in The National Archives in series RG 4 and indexed on the Mormon website **www.familysearch.org** and in digitised form at **www.bmdregisters.co.uk**) with the known registrations of meetings (again at The National Archives, this time in series RG 31) is depressing. In most counties there were dozens, even hundreds, of meetings registered for which no surviving records are known.

Between 1700 and about 1760 Nonconformist numbers decreased, but they rose again later in that century and increased dramatically when John Wesley's Methodists came out of the Church of England and became a separate organisation in the 1780s. They, too, were well organised and fairly centralised, and quickly began to keep records.

In the 19th century Nonconformist numbers grew dramatically, but general church attendance began to decline.

After the Reformation, the barometer of prejudice against Catholics (often known as "recusants" in this period) rose and fell according to the beliefs of the monarch and political expediency. Between 1559 and 1778 Roman Catholic services were illegal in England and Wales, and for nearly three centuries English law discriminated against them. Like Nonconformists, they could be required to appear before Quarter Sessions for non-attendance at church. For ordinary Catholics there may be no specifically Catholic records before about 1750, although they appear in all the standard non-religious sources. Their own records mostly relate to the clergy, their families and the actions of those who helped them.

In Europe, conflict between Protestants and the Catholic Church led groups of **Huguenots** (French Protestants) to flee persecution. Over two centuries some quarter of a million refugees, mainly from France and the Low Countries, sailed for England and Ireland. The first wave came over around 1520, and while some anglicised their names others retained their original family surname.

After being expelled from England in 1290, **Jews** were legally allowed back in 1656 and built their first synagogue, Bevis Marks, in the City of London in 1670. By the Second World War, Anglo-Jewry numbers reached a peak of half a million. Since then numbers have fallen through inter-marriage with non-Jews and emigration to Israel.

Until the 20th century the number of other non-Christians was a tiny proportion of the population. Almost all were temporary residents or new arrivals from abroad, and the vast majority were men. At various times there were quite a number, usually concentrated in London or the major ports, including Bristol and, later, Liverpool. If they married and founded families, their children and descendants almost certainly became Christian within a generation.

Many, however, were transitory, and in the 17th and 18th centuries numbers were very low. By the mid- and late 19th century there were many thousands overall, but they can be difficult to identify. Fortunately we do not have to identify an entire group, merely to recognise whether specific relatives of ours fall into any of the likely categories.

Here a word of warning. Often family myths have developed based on an odd surname, or generalisations about a common one, and the family have guessed themselves into being French, German or Jewish (the three most usual suspects).

However, the vast majority of British people's ancestors were in Britain at least as far back as 1600 and were Christian, mostly Anglican. If you have evidence that your ancestor was one of many other possibilities, obviously you must go with that, but otherwise it is sensible to assume the vastly more probable option.

A number of British people were converted (most not through any formal ceremony) to some form of the wisdom of the East, and from the 1880s the work of people such as the **Theosophists** spread among a certain stratum of the middle class. This ran parallel to the development of **Spiritualism**, which was sometimes based on Eastern philosophy and sometimes an outcrop of Christianity. In practice, these transformed the lives of individuals, but did not lead to congregations of families. Many people were willing to cherry-pick, largely from forms of **Buddhism**, but no substantial body of Asian Buddhists settled in this country up to the Second World War.

Until recently, the only large group of families in England with non-Christian customs were the **gypsies**, although they did not form religious congregations or maintain any independent religious records. To trace them we are dependent on the standard records of Anglican genealogy.

Some people nowadays would want to claim **witches** or **wiccans** or **druids** as having a separate religion. However, between 1500 and 1940 witches were seen as an evil form of Christianity, in contrast to herbalists and healers who practised legitimate folk cures.

The main part of this article was taken from Michael Gandy's *Cultures and Faiths: How your ancestors lived and worshipped* (The National Archives, 2007).

Handy Hints

There have been articles on tracing Catholics in issue 39; Methodists in issue 60 and Jewish burials in issue 43 of *Ancestors*.

USEFUL SOURCES FOR RELIGIOUS RESEARCH

Church of England parish records, plus records from Nonconformist chapels (from the early Victorian period), are generally held by local record offices. You can check many of these on the International Genealogical Index at **www.familysearch.org**.

In addition, the following archives may be able to help further:
Methodist Archives and Research Centre, John Rylands University Library, 150 Deansgate, Manchester M3 3EH; telephone 0161 275 3764; **www.library.manchester.ac.uk/specialcollections/collections/methodist**.

Religious Society of Friends (Quakers), Friends' House, 173–177 Euston Road, London NW1 2BJ; telephone 020 7663 1136; **www.quaker.org.uk**.

Catholic National Library, St Michael's Abbey, Farnborough Road, Farnborough GU14 7NQ; telephone 01252 546105; **www.catholic-library.org.uk**.

Catholic Family History Society; **www.catholic-history.org.uk/cfhs**

The Huguenot Society of Great Britain and Ireland, Huguenot Library, University of London, Gower Street, London WC1; telephone 020 7679 5199; **www.huguenotsociety.org.uk**.

The Jewish Genealogical Society of Great Britain, PO Box 13288, London N3 3WD; **www.jgsgb.org.uk**.

It is also worth looking at **www..movinghere.org.uk**.

Insightful INSCRIPTIONS

There is a wealth of genealogical information in local graveyards. **Richard Smart** unearths ways of finding whether your ancestors have been commemorated by a memorial inscription

Gravestones and their lettering are a visible part of our heritage in town and country churchyards, yet memorial inscriptions (MIs) must be the most familiar, but least celebrated, of all family history resources.

MIs can provide vital clues, particularly for the years before civil registration of births, marriages and deaths (BMDs) began in 1837, and censuses from 1841.

Before then, the most important source of information is parish registers of baptisms, marriages, and burials, although pre-1812 the amount of information varies widely. An MI, however, may often record a whole family, with their relationships to each other clearly stated, so you can draw up a genealogical tree with confidence.

Yet they are rarely used, probably because they are difficult to locate; there is no single archive or website you can search. In addition, only a very small proportion of burials are

marked by gravestones and inscriptions. A survey by the National Archive of Memorial Inscriptions (NAOMI) for Bedfordshire parishes revealed that only about one in eight burials have permanent memorials. The majority of earlier ones were in unmarked graves, or represented only by a wooden cross or headboard – ordinary people could not afford anything more durable – which have not survived.

Think of an old parish churchyard you know; then imagine it with nine or 10 times the number of stones it contains now to give an idea of how densely packed with the mortal remains of the parishioners it must be.

A good start for the family historian is the National Burial Index (NBI) – available at local record offices and family history society research centres – which contains over 10 million records, from which you may be able to locate a place of burial. Much of it is viewable online, using the newest technology – the internet – to preserve and publish to a global audience information recorded by the oldest technology – that of carving letters in stone. At present it is being transferred from Family History Online (**www.familyhistoryonline.co.uk**) to Findmypast (**www.findmypast.com**), so for a while you may have to visit both sites.

You can follow this up by contacting the

relevant family history society to find out whether there is an inscription transcript available. You will find contact details on the Federation of Family History Societies website at **www.ffhs.org.uk**. The amount of data available varies widely from society to society;

William Saunders's painting of St Mary's Church in Smeeth, near Ashford in 1853.

Kent Archaeological Society

The Kent Archaeological Society's website (**www.kentarchaeology.org.uk**) now offers nearly 16,000 pages of indexed records that can be searched and downloaded free of charge.

Among them are hundreds of memorial inscriptions that were transcribed in Kent parish churches and graveyards as long ago as 250 years ago, and since then have, in many cases, been destroyed or become illegible.

The earliest transcriptions were made in 1756–1760 by Rev Bryan Faussett. His work and notes on the history and architecture of the 115 East Kent churches he visited were donated to the Society of Antiquaries, and transcribed in longhand into six large notebooks by the Rev VJ Torr in the 1940s. Volunteers are now completing the task of making digital transcriptions of the notebooks for the KAS website.

Another antiquarian, Leland Lewis Duncan, transcribed MIs in about 150 West Kent parish churches between 1880 and 1923. His unpublished notes and a collection of other papers have also been digitally transcribed for the website.

The record of the memorial inscription for Mary Scott of Smeeth, Kent, who died in 1652.

NATIONAL ARCHIVE OF MEMORIAL INSCRIPTIONS (NAOMI)

Getting access to MIs in general is a problem. It was partly to remedy this that, in 2002, the Heritage Lottery Fund (HLF) agreed to support the setting up of NAOMI at the University of Bedfordshire.

The results of their work appear on **www.memorialinscriptions.org.uk**, which lets you search names, dates and/or places, with the results appearing as a summary of one line per person. Selecting any of these provides the following information free of charge: forename(s), surname, county, burial ground and the date of death (date, month, year). For £4 the full inscription can be downloaded, together with up to three other pieces of information for an extra £1 each if required and available – perhaps a photograph of the church, some historical text about the place and/or church, and a plan of the churchyard.

The NAOMI site addresses the problem of accessibility, and will become more successful as the database grows. Even though it is in its infancy, and as yet only includes two counties, it is already a large site which is an archive, not simply an index, and we are confident that the data is as reliable as possible.

They only accept data from reputable sources, (generally family history societies), and before uploading every entry is checked, using parish registers or births, marriages and deaths data if there is a problem, and then formatted.

Research suggests that about 38 per cent, or about 2.8 million inscriptions, have been transcribed, so an enormous archive of family history information has been saved for posterity. This also means that some 4.7 million have not been recorded, and thus are vulnerable. If we apply the survey's rate of loss it appears that we are losing some 23,500 inscriptions every year, or about 450 MIs per week.

As well as raising public awareness of the scale of the problem, NAOMI has also assisted groups in Norfolk and Bedfordshire in recording MIs. It has produced a complimentary DVD and a surveyors' handbook, which explains why it is important to record MIs and how to go about it. If you would like a copy please get in touch via their website.

some (such as Cornwall and Wiltshire) have recorded almost all their MIs, some only a few. Look under "memorial" or "monumental inscriptions" and try searching pages labelled "publications", "bookshop", "research", or "projects". The quality of the information varies, too. Some may just offer a summary of names and dates, some are merely indexes.

A very useful site which lists the addresses of MI related sites from all over the world is **www.framland.pwp.blueyonder.co.uk**.

INTERPRETING GRAVESTONES

OCCUPATION Some monuments will record the occupaton of the deceased.

DATES Not all inscriptions will record both dates of birth and death. Most will record the year of death and the age at the time of death.

OFFSPRING These are also recorded on graves stones along with the first and middle names.

NAMES The first name recorded on a gravestone is normally the first person in the family to die. These are usually the parents followed by children.

CAUSE Occasionally the cause of death is recorded. In this case, a mining accident. This should also be recorded in the local newspaper along with an account of the accident, particularly if others were also killed.

A view of Errigal old graveyard in County Tyrone.

IRISH GRAVES

The organisation of online Irish inscriptions is more centralised that those in Britain. The History from Headstones project website at **www.historyfromheadstones.com**, offers the largest collection of online inscriptions in Northern Ireland. It holds details of 50,000 inscriptions on gravestones, from over 800 graveyards in counties Antrim, Armagh, Down, Fermanagh, Londonderry and Tyrone. They can be downloaded for £4 each or £2 if you are a member of the Ulster Historical Guild (details at **www.ancestryireland.com**).

The largest Irish gravestone database is Ireland's Gravestone Index which can be found be clicking the Gravestone link at **www.irishgenealogy.ie**. It includes inscriptions from 851 cemeteries in ten counties. It is free to search the index but a charge is made to order the full text of the inscriptions.

SCOTTISH GRAVES

Scottish genealogy societies are also organising gravestone transcription projects, although most of this is available in printed form. However, there are a few online searches that can also done. The Aberdeen and North-East Scotland Family History Society – **www.ayrshireancestors.co.uk** – has an online index of its published inscriptions covering Aberdeen, Banffshire, Kincardineshire and Moray. The inscriptions have been taken from around 90 different burial grounds amounting to over 120,000 names.

For those with ancestors in Edinburgh, **www.edinburghancestors.org.uk** has a searchable database for gravestones in the city. There are around 50,000 entries in this database.

WORTH RECORDING

MIs are too important to lose. Apart from wills, they are the only public source of family history which is stamped by those whom it directly involves – often the deceased may have expressed his or her wishes about the form of the memorial and its wording. All other major public sources are "created" by someone else – parish records by the incumbent, BMD certificates and census returns by the registrar or enumerator, bounded by the design of the form on which the information was recorded. Every MI is unique – a public expression of the deepest of private feelings about love, grief, loss, and faith.

We owe it to our successors to take note of the verse quoted on the cover of Jeremy Jones's excellent booklet, *How to Record Graveyards* (CBA and Rescue, 1976): "Preserve these stones, avert the crime / Snatch history from the hands of time."

MILITARY GRAVES

For those with military ancestors who were killed in either of the world wars, there is really only one place to start looking online – The Commonwealth War Graves Commission website – **www.cwgc.org**.

The CWGC is a non-profit-making organisation which gives details of the final resting places, or where the names were recorded, of 1.7 million men and women from the Commonwealth forces who died during both world wars. Their online site is free to search and contains photographs of the cemeteries where soldiers are buried or commemorated.

WHY CAN'T I FIND THEM?

Don't be downhearted when you seem to have reached the end of the line in your researches. **Michael Gandy** suggests ways around the brick wall

Most family historians are always stuck because as soon as we solve one problem, we move on to the next. When was he born? When did the parents marry? Where had they come from? When did they die?

The problems should be an interesting challenge; but we all like to be successful sooner rather than later, so it can be frustrating when all avenues seem to have been explored.

Fortunately many of the new indexes which have come out over the last few years – for example, census entries or First World War medal cards – are available online, meaning that we can often solve problems pretty well at the click of a mouse.

But what do you do when all the material has been indexed, and your people still aren't there?

Analyse the problem

Working out exactly what the problem is should give you a clue as to the direction you need to follow.

■ Sometimes we may have no idea where the ancestors were, but they have such distinctive names, we shall recognise them the minute we find them.

■ Sometimes we know perfectly well where they should be, but can't find them in the records.

■ Sometimes, when they have common names or occupations, we find lots of people who look like them, but don't know which are the right ones.

Cast your net wider

If the names are distinctive, then work systematically through the likely records. Make a shopping list of the right sources and the order in which to search them.

If they are all unindexed, then work through the sources one by one. Where some are indexed or transcribed, or online, then it doesn't hurt to start with the most accessible – so long as you remember that the sources you looked at first were not actually at the top of your list.

When indexes don't contain entries you were confident would be there, be prepared to go through the originals yourself. Indexes are wonderful – but they aren't perfect.

Census records for the Fordham family, listing William, Hannah and James under their step-father's name. William was the father of Lilian, the author's grandmother.

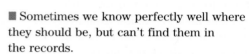

William	Do.	Son		10		Do.	Kent Plumstead
Henry	Do.	Son		15 mo.			Kent Plumstead
Charles Patey		Head	Mar	21	Bricklayers Labourer		Kent Bexley
Jane	Do.	Wife	Mar	19			Kent East Wickham
Jane	Do.	Daug	–	3 mo.	–		Kent Bexley Heath
James Fordham		Head	Mar	30	Agricultural Labourer		Kent, East Wickham
Mary Ann	Do.	Wife	Mar	40	Hawker		Kent, Bexley
William	Do.	Son		16	Bakers labourer		Kent Woolwich
Hannah	Do.	Daugh	–	14	Scholar		Kent Northfleet
James	Do.	Son	–	9	Scholar		Kent Erith
Jane	Do.	Daug	–	6			Kent Crayford

TNA RG 11/861

However, first try to think of other possibilities that the names might have been indexed under.

Sometimes there are transcription errors – understandable ones when the handwriting is bad, or less understandable ones, like my grandmother Lilian, who was transcribed as William despite being clearly described as a daughter!

Sometimes the fault lies in the source. Lilian's father was a Beckett but he and his sisters appear in one census as Fordham, which was the name of their step-father. Perhaps Mrs Fordham detailed her husband and then her children and never thought to mention that the first three children were by her first husband. So the enumerator just put ditto marks all down the page.

The same applies to places. A man may give Pimlico as his birthplace in one census and Westminster in the next and both would be right.

Some of my wife's railway relatives seemed to have moved from Wolverton, Buckinghamshire, to a place called Monks Coppenhall in Cheshire, which turned out to be the old name for Crewe.

On different occasions, the same people from the same few streets in and near the South Lambeth Road, in South London have their birthplaces as given as Lambeth, Nine Elms, Vauxhall, Kennington, Stockwell and Clapham. For all I know there may be other entries giving birthplaces I haven't thought of, such as The Oval.

Try to work out the indexer's policy on variants. Some indexes group them all together; others keep them separate with or without cross-references. When you ask some computer indexes for "Frederick" they may not bring up Fred or Fredk or Freddie. Clark and Clarke may be indexed separately without a link. Use the wild card (symbols such as * or ?) whenever you can.

Be sure to note whether any sources are missing. There is a world of difference between knowing you have looked at everything – or just everything that survived.

If you get stuck on a particular ancestor it helps to look around for people who might be related, people with the same names (especially uncommon ones), working at the same occupation, living in the same place, attending the same chapel.

People nearby may well be married sisters, elderly parents, uncles, aunts or cousins – if you could only recognise them.

Even neighbours may have come to the area at about the same time for the same reason – and from the same place.

It always helps to do some background research. In the countryside, for example, find out who were the local gentry and landowners. If they were new to the area they may have

Gardeners employed on a Burton on Trent estate in 1880. It is likely their children were also employed at the local great houses.

imported workers from back home. If they had relatives who were big employers in an industrial town they may have recommended anyone leaving the village to go there, giving them a letter of recommendation for a job.

It also helps to trace the family sideways. In real life relatives include lots of people connected by marriage or remarriage. You may see more of your daughter-in-law's family than you do of your own, and know your son-in-law's sisters better than your nieces.

Large families of the past offer even more complicated possibilities. His brother married her sister. The grandson married a niece of the stepmother. The older sister married her brother-in-law's widowed father. The younger son was apprenticed to his stepmother's brother.

Close relationships like this were vital, but may be invisible to the family historian who sticks strictly to blood lines.

What's in a name?

Many people who research the origin of their surname start off knowing that "it's a Kent name". This can do more harm than good if it leads you to believe that the answer to your problem probably lies in Kent.

English surnames originated in the 1200s (a bit later in the North and rather later in Wales) and your line may have moved to Hampshire in the 1400s and then to Oxfordshire in the 1600s before coming to London in the 1800s.

Most of us don't live where our grandparents did. Even during the 19th century most of them didn't live where their grandparents did. People have always moved about.

If your ancestor has a fairly uncommon name, then other families giving the same Christian names may be related. But beware! Biblical names, for example, aren't that uncommon, especially in the North of England, and a Moses in 1850 doesn't have to be descended from a 1650 Moses. Both families may simply have been Bible-reading Christians.

Some "Biblical" names are not purely Biblical. Jeremiah, for example, was very common among Catholic Irish, and is the real name of many men called Jerry.

Names may relate to particular areas. Cuthbert, for example, is found fairly often in the North East but far less frequently

The late Queen Mother was a Bowes-Lyon before her marriage to Prince Albert in 1923; but if you find an ancestor with a similar surname it doesn't necessarily mean you are related to royalty.

elsewhere. Lewis is rare in England but quite common in Wales.

Other names were a passing fashion. Children called Horatio or Gladstone (or Elvis) show us something about their parents' interests but nothing about their relations.

Certain names have a very specific local connection. In a parish where I have ancestors a lot of girls were called Theodosia for a while. They were named after a local lady who was presumably either greatly liked or very happy to be a godmother – no doubt giving a generous christening present.

Most Christian names are so common that no theory can be built on them. "Look, they must be related because they both had a son called John and daughter called Mary!" Sadly, not.

Beware of looking for your surname in books of famous people or the aristocracy. Most surnames are much more common than we think and a lot of people are hypnotised by knowing that Lord So-and-So had a coat-of-arms (so that must be ours as well) and that they must be descended from a younger branch of that family ("because everyone's related if you go back far enough").

Spencer, Bowes and Lyons are all fairly common names (to take only the obvious names from the Royal Family), but if you have those names in your ancestry you aren't necessarily related to Diana Princess of Wales or the late Queen Mother. The Scots had a proverb: "Not every Stuart is a cousin of the King."

It helps to be realistic about social class and social mobility. Do a bit of hard thinking about how much your ancestors earned, what class they had, who would have invited them to tea and whom they would have told their children to keep away from.

Flora Thompson in *Lark Rise to Candleford* pinpoints the social problems of the schoolmistress – too good to take tea with the labourers; not good enough to take tea with a lady.

Some clues are false

There was always a Nathaniel. They were always Methodists. They were always butchers. The eldest boy was always named after the father. Alas, no.

Everything starts somewhere. There must have been a first Nathaniel, even if the name came from outside the family. Somebody decided to be a Methodist. The farmer decided to apprentice his youngest son to a butcher.

Members of the Wesleyan synod in Somerset in 1896. Some people attended a chapel because it was their nearest place of worship rather than through religious conviction.

Maybe they named the eldest boy after the grandfather, or a favourite brother who had died young, or an employer, or a good friend.

In Scotland the naming pattern is fairly tight, and one can expect the eldest few children to be named after specific relatives.

Ashkenazim Jews, they tell me, never name a child after anyone living but when someone dies the next child is likely to be given his or her name (or a similar name, say, one beginning with the same first letter, if the child is a different gender).

But in England there weren't any binding rules, and children's names depend on the feeling of the parents or pressure from relatives.

Religion, too, is a personal choice. Many children stick with the faith they were brought up in. Others change, perhaps to their husband or wife's religion, or because of their employer.

In the 19th century most Nonconformist sects had basically the same service format as Low Church Anglican churches, so many people were quite happy to go to the most convenient church without worrying too much about the label.

My grandmother knew perfectly well that her grandmother had changed the family's religion in 1863 when a Wesleyan Methodist chapel was built in their small village. Before, there had been a mile's walk with a growing family; now it was only a hundred yards.

Many parents, of course, did not attend church regularly themselves but were naturally drawn to have their baptisms and marriages in the place where their children went to Sunday School.

As to occupation, all bets are off.

It is often said that in upper class families the eldest son had the land, the second went into the Army, the third into the Church and so on, which may be true: at least sometimes.

In more ordinary families, too, there would be a tendency for some of the sons to go into the father's business because they knew how it worked and he had the connections.

But it is likely there were other relatives, friends or neighbours whom the parents could call on to help their children get started. And a boy with strong opinions and some gumption can organise his own life.

That said, a family does often stay in associated occupations.

Take Frederick Adams, who was a piano maker. By the 1901 census one son is in the same line while two others are a piano tuner and a piano hawker (although I don't suppose he actually took the pianos round with him from door to door) respectively. One of the grandsons was also a piano maker and two of the girls were music teachers.

On the other hand, Thomas Gandy was an engineer in a cotton mill, but his four sons all made boots and shoes (and clogs) and his son-in-law was a plumber.

In short, be open to all possibilities – but don't be open to all possibilities!

PRESERVING
PICTURES AND PAPERS

Leslie Cram explains how he archived some 4,000 family photographs, along with notes, diaries, letters and other documents onto his computer, discovering more about his ancestors in the process

Having spent 25 years working in museums, where we compiled catalogues onto computer databases, I wanted to do something similar at home. My aim was to make digital copies of the family photos in case anything happened to the originals, and so I could send copies to relatives and other interested individuals. I also wanted to catalogue a vast collection of family papers, which at the time were stored in 24 shoe boxes.

Using Microsoft Access I set up two databases, then devised my own system around them. If you have Microsoft programs on your computer you may already have Access.

My family photographic archive collection numbers just under 4,000. Prints, negatives and transparencies are housed in 18 A4 size, loose leaf, spring binders in plastic sleeves, which have pockets of varying sizes to take the originals, as well as any negatives. In addition,

there is a box of 100 old glass quarter-plate negatives.

The spring binders are in three series: my mother's side of the family up to her marriage; my father's side up to his marriage, and then their combined life. For each child every photograph is included up to the time when he or she left home. After that they have their own collection. The albums continue to hold all images of my parents, plus family occasions such as weddings, funerals and Christmas gatherings up to the present day. Within these three series the photographs are stored in chronological order. Information is written on the back of the picture or on slips of paper in its pocket.

Work on the collection began when my parents were still alive. My mother trained as a surgeon and then worked in a Methodist hospital in Wuhan in central China in the 1930s, even keeping the hospital going during the Japanese occupation. My father was a Methodist missionary who worked in rural areas. My parents married in China in 1939, later moving to Vancouver, British Columbia

Medical staff at the Methodist hospital, Hankow, China, around 1935, where Dr Mary Redhead, the author's mother, was a surgeon. She sits on the left of Dr Chiang, head of the hospital, in the front row.

for four years. After a few years in England they returned to central China in 1945, staying until 1949, when the family finally returned to Britain after the Communist revolution.

They both kept good photographic records of their time in China and Canada. They had put the pictures into albums, with full details written beside or on the back of prints, and were happy to check anything that was unclear to me.

Then there were the earlier photographs of grandparents and great-grandparents, going back to the 1870s. On both sides of the family there was an aunt who held these, and who was delighted to help. I took copies using a conventional SLR camera, while they supplied the information, all then stored in order in the binders.

After collecting everything I could from my parents and the two aunts, I started visiting other family members, taking the binders with me and asking whether they had any more information on the existing photos, or other photos which I could copy. I even went to see a Canadian cousin, who had not known before that his father had had an elder brother – my mother's father.

I entered the data by following the existing chronological order of the photographs in the binders. Access assigned a new sequential number for each new entry, which was also written on the back of the photograph.

The first fields were concerned with identification of the individuals. First, family surname was followed by boxes for entering family members with that surname, identified using their full forenames. A female was entered using her maiden surname up to marriage, then her new surname after marriage. Then the second family surname was entered with two boxes for forenames of that family. Finally I created a third family surname and one forename box.

Next, the year, the day and the month were entered as far as known. The country, the place and the address followed. A field for the occasion is valuable in searching. My personal classification included wedding, funeral, seaside, countryside, river, garden, portrait, studio portrait, family group, and others. A field for "description" included any information not already entered, such as whose wedding it is. The "taken by" field had an entry when it was known. The "reverse" field was filled in when the image was of the back of the photograph with interesting writing or a commercial stamp. "Associated documentation" held the actual text on the back of the photograph or in an album, with the "location" field saying where the text was.

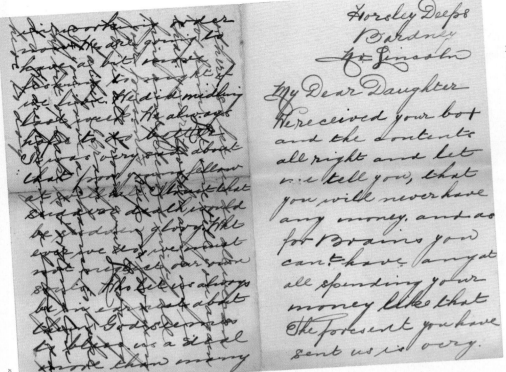

Author

A letter written by Isaac Cram in 1904 to his daughter, Lucy. On the left page you can see the common practice of the time of writing in two directions across a piece of paper to save space.

The "note" field took any information left over.

Finally, the "reference" field took the number associated with the photograph, usually the batch number of the prints from one film. Where there was no batch number, but it was clear that prints came from a single film, a batch number was made up, so prints from the same film were always kept together.

When it came to digitising the pictures, black and white photographs were scanned in at 300 dpi and 8-bit greyscale, colour photographs at 600 dpi and 24-bit colour. If you have a scanner at home it should be able to do all this easily. The scanner took prints up to A4 size, transparencies, plastic negatives from 35 mm to 55mm by 85 mm and glass quarter plate negatives. The image was saved as a tiff (alternatively as a jpeg).

The images were copied onto 700mb compact discs (CD), then deleted from the computer to release memory. One series of CDs holds the images burnt on in a recordable read-only CDR format that cannot be tampered with. Another series of CDs has the images in read-write or CDRW format which allows editing. This second CDRW series is the master where mistakes are corrected when found.

There are 19 discs totalling some 12 gigabytes of memory but, inevitably, our present CDs and computers will become obsolete, so in the long term it is the 18 binders holding the originals which may survive to be the usable images, together with a paper copy of the database.

When it came to tackling the mammoth collection of family papers, I was faced with 24 shoeboxes containing notes, diaries, postcards, family letters and even an autobiography of my Primitive Methodist minister forebears written in 1910. The earliest document, dating back to 1879, is my father's mother's certificate in religious knowledge. There are 265 postcards and 28 letters from 1894 to 1911, kept by my father's grandfather's family. On my mother's side, there are diaries from 1881 and 1901.

In the mid-1880s some of her ancestors emigrated to New Zealand, while others became missionaries in Africa. According to family legend, two of the missionaries' children were eaten by crocodiles, but this was disproved by a letter which unromantically states that they drowned in the Vaal River.

The archive becomes more exotic in the 1930s, when my parents were sending back letters and papers from their work in China. For a time, my father was the only foreigner in the district, and was in charge of refugees under the Japanese occupation. The diaries he kept from 1931 until his death in 1998 are all in the archive.

From 1959, as the children began to leave home, there are papers from New Zealand, the United States, Australia, Canada, Germany, France, and Ethiopia.

After their deaths, my parents' papers were collected together and I sorted them into rough chronological order in special archive boxes. I then arranged them in three series, as I had already done for the photographs.

I now took the boxes one at a time, from the earliest to latest, sorted the papers within into strict chronological order and then started to list each piece of paper.

For this catalogue I built a second database with 15 fields. This is easier to use than a single database with 40 fields, and anyway, Access allows you to search two databases almost as easily as just one.

I referred to my family tree when checking exact names, dates and locations of events described in the papers, so everything tallied.

The database begins with a unique number, starting from one; the program then generating the next number as the cataloguing process continues. After that comes the field for "format" which records whether the paper is a certificate, diary, letter, postcard, telegram, and so on.

Then there are two fields for who generated the paper, by surname, then Christian name or names. As with the photographs; an individual is identified using his or her full Christian names. A woman is entered using her maiden surname up to marriage, then new surname after marriage. To differentiate between a mother and daughter both called Lucy, the birth surname is added in brackets. The following two fields show the recipient of the document. The next four fields give the date by year, month and day, followed by "action" – which records whether the paper was written, postmarked, or signed etc on that date. The "country" field denotes where the paper was generated, with the address giving the village, town or city. "Content" contains a summary of the paper. The "notes" field includes where the paper had recently been stored, related papers, number of sheets and similar information. Lastly, "store" notes in which box the paper can be found.

My next move was to write the unique number onto the paper or papers with a soft pencil in the top right hand corner. While every photograph is a single image, a document may consist of a number of sheets, for instance a letter or a diary. Rather than giving each page a unique number, I assigned a single number to the whole document, which meant sometimes putting letters written by an individual over one year into a bundle that might be two inches thick. Each uniquely numbered paper or papers was stored in its own see-through, acid-free plastic sleeve. This keeps all the sheets of a multiple-page letter together.

Plastic sleeves with punched holes are stored in numerical sequence in A4 ring binders. Larger papers are stored in individual sleeves. Everything from one series was then stored in an archive box, while papers larger than the boxes are held in A3 folders.

Anyone using the archive has to abide by the rule of only opening one box at one time to avoid the possibility of mixing sheets, and papers are stored flat, never folded, so there is no bending and unbending of the document, which reduces its life.

We also transcribed spoken memories of relatives – some recorded by my aunt, some by my father – and added the typescripts to the collection.

There are about 1,800 unique numbers in

the archive, ranging in size from a 1941 Honolulu bus ticket to my mother's 27-page account of the Japanese takeover of Wuhan in 1938.

I estimate the total number of pages in the collection at around 10,000, which is why, unlike the photographs, the papers were not copied.

However, I am giving a catalogue to my relatives and interested institutions, telling them I can make copies of originals if asked.

I had expected to uncover at least one illegitimate birth or other family secrets. But in fact, there was nothing except deeper insight into events and personalities.

For instance, my mother's sister spoke of her father, a Primitive Methodist minister, going to the local Anglican vicar with the body of his first-born child named John, who had died at birth. The vicar had refused burial as was the custom of the Anglican Church at that time because the baby had not been baptised.

This accounts for the two and a half years between her parents' marriage and my mother's birth as the eldest surviving child. It also gives an explanation for the strength with which my mother pursued opportunities and the difficult relationship she had with her mother (who may have resented my mother living in the place of the first-born son).

My mother never spoke of this, and I shall never know now what is the truth; but I have a deeper sense of what was at the heart of how she lived her life.

HERE TO HELP

Sitting in front of a computer or poring over old documents may seem a rather solitary pastime, but you need not feel alone

There are some key organisations in the world of family history which can help solve your problems, offer advice and ideas, or just give you the chance to meet other enthusiasts. Whether you are not sure which records to use or need to buy a piece of software, there is almost bound to be somebody who has been there before you.

Family history societies

Every county – and some cities and towns – in Great Britain now has at least one family history society. They are run by volunteers who often have an amazing, in-depth knowledge of the district and its people. Some are also doing invaluable work transcribing and indexing local documents.

Most societies keep in touch with their members through a quarterly journal featuring historical articles about life in the area, local records or archives, and local news. They also list members' interests, which allows people to share research.

Societies hold regular meetings, usually consisting of a lecture given by an expert on some aspect of family or local history. Many groups publish books, CDs and online data

relating to the communities they cover, and meetings often include a bookstall where you can see the latest publications. Most organise day schools, conferences and fairs that will help extend your level of expertise as well as being interesting and extremely entertaining. Look out for details on *Ancestors* news pages.

Although societies do not usually have the resources to undertake research on your behalf, some offer look-up services, usually for a small fee or donation. Larger groups may run their own research centres, where you can use general family history sources, transcribed records, indexes, and sometimes local historical material. These centres are normally free to members, with a small charge for non-members.

It is well worth joining the society in the neighbourhood where you live or work, even if you don't have any genealogical interests in the area. Once you are established with your research and have a good idea where your ancestral home was, you could join the society for that district as well.

Guild of One-Name Studies

Another type of local society focuses on a particular name or variants of it. In such one-name studies researchers look at how the geographical distribution of a particular name changes over the centuries, or attempt to reconstruct the genealogy of as many lines as possible bearing the name.

As an umbrella organisation, the Guild of One Name Studies maintains a register which allows you to discover whether anyone is undertaking a study on any of "your" surnames. It also brings together those with an interest in other forms of surname study, such as DNA projects. The Guild has over 2,000 members spread across the world, studying over 7,500 individual surnames.

Many members register a surname so as to embark on a Guild-recognised one-name study, and co-ordinate worldwide activity in studying that particular name. Only one person may register a specific surname, but membership of the Guild is open to anyone with an interest in the subject, and it is not restricted to those

Members of the Family and Community History Research Society visit the Merchant Adventurer's Almshouse in York.

---

who just wish to register a name.

If you have a surname in your family being studied by a Guild member then they may well be able to provide you with valuable information, and perhaps your own connection with it. You can find out which surnames are being studied from the online register, along with contact details.

Details at **www.one-name.org.uk** or write to the Guild of One-Name Studies, Box G, 14 Charterhouse Buildings, Goswell Road, London EC1M 7BA.

Society of Genealogists

Stocked with books, indexes and guides on four cramped floors in central London, the Society of Genealogists' (SoG) library holds all the sources you would expect – plus some less well known treasures.

Examples of every type of family history record you have ever used or heard of can be found somewhere in the library's four floors, interspersed with more specialist and obscure sources that you will probably have never come across before. Its website includes a catalogue of its holdings at **www.sog.org.uk/sogcat/sogcat.shtml**.

The Society is keen to cater for every kind of family historian, be they beginners who are initially looking at the bread and butter sources (such as parish registers, directories and poll books), or the more advanced who may be using its extensive collection of school histories or overseas records.

It has the best collection of records for British citizens who worked or lived abroad, for example in the United States, Australia and India, outside the British Library. It also has many rare shipping lists, pre-1920 adoption papers, films, and one of the best collections of regimental histories outside the National Army Museum.

In addition, the SoG holds the Bank of England's pre-1845 will extracts submitted by shareholders, including the executors of Horatio Nelson's will dated 1805. They feature the names of beneficiaries along with the stocks and shares which were to be left to them.

Over the years the Society has also acquired thousands of family trees and roll pedigrees, as well as collections of notes from people's researches.

The Society of Genealogists's Genealogy Officer Else Churchill with a family tree from the Society's collection.

Some of the SoG's most prized treasures are trees dating back to the 1700s, ornately decorated with crests and illustrations.

Visitors to its headquarters can use an internet suite with membership to sites such as FreeBMD, Ancestry, Origins, and Findmypast for free. In addition, it is at present trialling free access to The National Archives's Documents Online service. For technophobes, or those who are simply new to genealogy, the Society also runs regular computer tutorials looking at particular types of software or how to make the best use of the internet. These are part of a diverse programme of courses and seminars which it runs to build up the skills of family historians, alongside regular lectures and workshops.

Family and Community History Research Society

Students, inspired by what they had practised on an Open University (OU) course on history, wanted to have something concrete upon which to build their future research, and thus was born the Family and Community History Research Society (FACHRS).

Over the past 10 years it has grown from being a practical way of organising national research, with a journal, *Family and Community History*, linking academic historians with amateurs, to an organisation that is now recognised as a valuable contributor to historical research. It's best known for running collaborative projects involving members who each contribute their research to an academic co-ordinator.

Currently, the Society is running a major research project on almshouses in collaboration with the Local Population Studies Society. There are also several mini-projects on the go, such as checking Victorian marriage registers to determine their reliability, and researching the lives of individual household servants using census enumerators' books.

The Society runs a continued learning programme, with sessions on subjects such as "Using a database in Historical Research", "Researching Village Communities", and "Writing for your Journal".

More details at **www.fachrs.com**.

Searching for
MAPS ONLINE

Maps are valuable tools for family and local historians alike. **David McVey** guides you to some of his favourite cartographic websites

A map of Cheam, Morden and Nonsuch Park dating to the reign of Edward VI produced before the Court of Augmentations. It concerns common and intercommoning rights within a waste common called Sparrow Field.

Everybody lived somewhere and worked somewhere. So whether your research remains local or hurtles to a distant corner of the country, it will still be grounded in place, which means you will need to consult maps.

While there's nothing to beat poring over old maps in a library or archive, today an increasingly vast range of cartographic material is digitised and available online.

A useful starting point is two sources of contemporary Ordnance Survey (OS) maps, Multimap and Streetmap, to be found at **www.multimap.co.uk** and **www.streetmap.co.uk** respectively. Both provide recent OS mapping extracts with a choice of scales, and you can search for postcodes, street names or place names.

The OS's Get-a-map search facility will

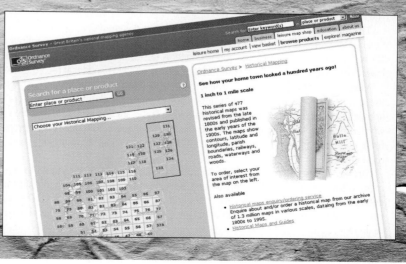

help you match place to map. However, in my experience, Streetmap's system is a little better at locating the names of single features or houses – an important detail for ancestry researchers.

Bear in mind that the maps will not necessarily be the absolute latest printings; if you need completely up-to-date material you can order the most recent editions online from the OS itself at **www.ordnancesurvey.co.uk**.

Another feature that may be of interest is the OS Select Map facility, which enables you to order a map centred on your home or other feature. This is useful if the family you are researching appear to have lived right on the edge or corner of several adjoining standard OS maps – an all too frequent occurrence.

The OS also produces a variety of printed historical maps which can be browsed at **http://leisure.ordnancesurvey.co.uk/leisure/ItemDetails.jsp?item=os_historical**.

They cover most of the country as it was roughly 100 years ago at 1:63,360 scale (1 inch to 1 mile), which is useful for comparing with today's 1:50,000 Landranger series.

The OS also has historical town maps dating from the early 19th century to the mid-20th century.

Another rich source is the Old Maps site, **www.old-maps.co.uk**, which claims to be "Britain's most extensive digital historical map archive" with 19th and 20th century 1:10,560 and 1:2,500 scale OS maps. You can zoom in and out of maps online, although the reproduction is not always all that good.

A useful facility is the ability to compare a modern OS map with the equivalent historical source.

British History Online has fascinating digitisations of some 18th and 19th century OS maps at both 1:2500 and 1:10,560 scale on

An example of a large scale Ordnance Survey map for Devonport about 1911.

www.british-history.ac.uk/map.asp.

Its coverage does not stretch to the whole of the UK, but if areas that interest you are on the maps, they are a fascinating resource. The 1:2500 maps in particular offer a remarkable amount of detail, down to the level of individual houses, streets and structures.

One of the most valuable lessons to be gained from comparing historical maps with contemporary ones is the way that place names evolve over time. I've recently been studying Antermony, a former country house and estate in what used to be Stirlingshire. In the 17th century and earlier, other variants such as "Auchtermony" appear; only by seeing where these names appear on historical maps can we be sure that they refer to the same place.

The British Library has, of course, a bewildering range of maps available; check out its catalogues on **www.bl.uk/collections/maps.html**. The site also has a useful series of guides to maps that are of particular value for tracing the history of, for example, buildings and houses.

The amount of material available digitised on the site is disappointingly small. However, there are several online exhibitions, including a number of the maps from the recent *London: a Life in Maps* show.

By contrast, the National Library of Scotland site has a wealth of online mapping resources at **www.nls.uk**. The digital map library is at **www.nls.uk/maps**.

There are various search options available, but a useful method is to choose a county and then do a geographical search to see what is available online.

For example, there are 13 options featuring

Using maps in your family history

The first maps date from the middle ages, although map-making as we know it, really dates from the 18th century. The Ordnance Survey was founded in 1791 to map the whole of the British Isles. Millions of maps survive – The National Archives alone has five million from around the world. Most local studies libraries and record offices have maps for their areas. There are four main types, which are likely to be of use:

Enclosure maps – were drawn up at a time when the land in a parish was enclosed (that is divided up among the local landowners). This usually happened between about 1750 and 1850. The maps show how the land was divided up and there are accompanying schedules showing who owned what parcels of land. Incomplete sets are held at The National Archives and local record offices.

Tithe maps – also relate to property ownership and were drawn up under the Tithe Commutation Act 1836, to assess the amount of tax due to be paid to the Anglican church. The maps and the accompanying apportionments (assessments) indicate how much land an individual owned. Again, incomplete sets are held at the PRO and local record offices.

Valuation Office maps – are little known – little wonder because they are difficult to use, but persevere as they are full of fascinating information about the houses your ancestors lived in just before the First World War. The maps and related field books, all of which are at The National Archives, were drawn up between 1911 and 1916 in preparation for a land tax, and contain detailed descriptions of most properties in urban as well as rural areas.

Ordnance Survey maps – began by publishing the famous inch-to-the-mile series of maps in the early years of the 19th century. By mid-century they had begun producing detailed surveys of towns, even down to indicating the location of lamposts. They can give you a good idea of the layout of an area. The National Archives has a reasonable collection, as do many local archives.

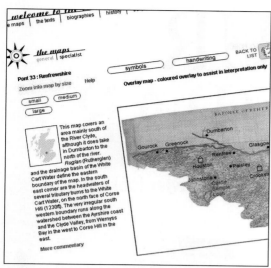

The digital map library is on www.nls.uk/maps

Several companies produce reproduction Ordnance Survey maps which are well worth buying if you are trying to work out where and how your ancestors lived. They are sold in local bookshops, and local record offices, and The National Archives bookshop has a very good selection. You can also buy them online:

Cassini Maps at **www.cassinimaps.co.uk** produce one-inch maps showing a particular county or area.

Alan Godfrey Maps at **www.alangodfreymaps.co.uk** produce large scale maps of late-Victorian and Edwardian towns and cities.

Stirlingshire. They date from Timothy Pont's hand-drawn maps of the late 16th century and the beautiful maps from Blaeu's *Atlas Novus* of 1654 which are based on Pont's work (incidentally, Antermony is rendered "Atermynny" in both of these); to 20th century Bartholomew and OS maps, where the newly-demolished Antermony House is no longer shown.

The whole history of a building or landscape can be traced – as long as it's in Scotland, anyway.

Within the Digital Mirror section of the National Library of Wales website at **www.llgc.org.uk/index.php?id=73**, there is a fascinating series of county maps, published in 1718 by Thomas Taylor of London. These have been taken from his atlas *The Principality of Wales Exactly Described* which, as far as anyone knows, is the first devoted entirely to Wales.

The National Archives has a small selection of digitised maps available at **www.nationalarchives.gov.uk/imagelibrary/maps**. For example, there's a beautiful map of part of the Irish coast from 1580, and a sketch-map of the area around Nonsuch Park, Surrey, from the time of Edward VI.

If you want to try a more general search, you can access what's held in the paper archives of all major UK research libraries through the facility at COPAC on **www.copac.ac.uk**. To look for maps, click the "ENTER COPAC" button and then choose "Map Search".

Numerous sites are gathered in a bewildering array of links at the Map History site's list of online historical maps at **www.maphistory.info**, which covers not just the UK but also the rest of the world. There are even suggestions of useful websites for family historians.

Similarly, Oxford's Bodleian Library signposts a wide range of map sites all round the world at **www.bodley.ox.ac.uk/users/nnj/maplinks.htm**.

It is also worth checking the website of your local archives, library, museum or college for online maps of local interests. Some counties also have collections of digitised maps; Cheshire is a particularly good example, at **http://maps.cheshire.gov.uk**.

At some point, you'll probably need to switch from virtual map research to consulting the real thing; but the above sites will allow you to find out what the libraries have available, or enable you to purchase copies of maps.

The tithe map drawn up for the parish of Boconnoc near Lostwithiel, Cornwall, 1838.

USING YOUR
LOCAL LIBRARY

Libraries offer far more than just books these days. **Simon Fowler** looks at how family historians can use their online services

If you are not already a member of your local library, now is the time to join. Membership, which is normally free, allows you to borrow books and much else, as well as letting you use their computers. You can even use your library card to access some sites from your home computer.

Check which online services your branch subscribes to by visiting the library pages on your council's website. A quick survey suggests that almost all provide some facilities, usually the online version of the Oxford Dictionary of National Biography (DNB) and other Oxford University Press services. About half also offer access to The Times Digital Archive. These are two major research sources for genealogists.

In addition, many libraries subscribe to the databases provided by the Ancestry family history websites (particularly **www.ancestry.co.uk**), although these can only be used in the library itself.

You can see a complete list of links to public library websites around the UK at **http://dspace.dial.pipex.com/town/square/ac940/weblibs.html**. This site will also tell you whether your local library has an online catalogue to its holdings, and whether it has digitised any old photograph collections.

The *Oxford DNB* consists of short biographies of over 55,000 people who have shaped Britain's past over the last 2,400 years – from Julius Caesar and Boudicca, to Princess Diana and Sid Vicious, and from the founding fathers of America, to the nawabs of Bengal.

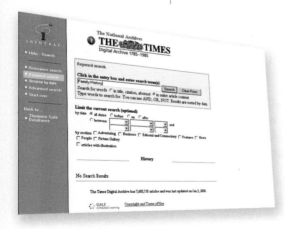

The famous, the infamous and the just plain eccentric all merit entries. The website provides the full text of the 60-volume print edition, over 10,000 illustrations, an expanding range of invaluable reference lists, plus articles on themes and groups and, where appropriate, links to The National Archives's National Register of Archives (see page 34).

It is possible to do a full-text search by word or phrase, but clearly the DNB is of most help to people related to any of the subjects whose lives it describes. It is also very useful if you come across a name – such as the general who commanded an ancestor's regiment – and you want to find out more.

Incidentally, the Know How service, to which most libraries also subscribe, includes *Who was Who*, which consists of short biographies of thousands of figures who are, or were, in the public eye during the 20th century. This is also now available on the Oxford DNB website.

To access *Oxford DNB* click on **www.oxforddnb.com/subscribed**. You will then be asked to input your library ticket details. To check whether your library is in the scheme, go to **www.oup.com/oxforddnb/info/freeodnb/libraries**.

The other major resource, The Times Digital Archive, covers two centuries of issues of *The Times*, from the date of its foundation on 1 January 1785 until the end of 1985. It is

Major Simon Frazer, 15th Lord Lovat, led a Commando unit during the Second World War. Here he is photographed briefing members of 4 Commando during Operation Abercromby, the raid on the French village of Hardelot, near Boulogne, on the night of 21 April 1942.

easy to use – just type in a name, place or phrase. You can narrow the search by date or by section, such as advertising, editorial or news. You can also read the whole issue for a particular date.

However, the search is not always 100 per cent comprehensive, and it can be difficult to print out pages, particularly for longer stories. In addition, despite its reputation as a paper of record, there are certain topics which *The Times* does not always cover as well – if indeed at all – as its more downmarket rivals, such as gory murders, disasters and celebrity scandals.

That said, at the peak of its prestige and influence in the 1840s and 1850s it published detailed, and sometimes stomach-turning accounts, of scandals such as the starving paupers in the Andover workhouse and the appalling conditions faced by soldiers in the Crimea. There is good coverage of London, including detailed reports from even minor courts.

Obituaries, which don't really start until well into the 19th century, were much less comprehensive or personal than we have

Above, his Oxford DNB entry, which describes him as: "Athletic, debonair, extremely courageous, and an inspiring leader, Shimi Lovat was also ruthless and intolerant of inefficiency in his army career. He was also erudite, intelligent, humorous, and shrewd."

become used to, but could still yield something of interest.

The advertising pages are a joy: entertainments and patent medicines, households seeking governesses and servants, notices of births, marriages and deaths plus, of course, the famous personal columns.

It is certainly worth typing in the names of your ancestors to see whether they appear, particularly if they were Londoners or had connections with the capital. It is also useful if you are studying a particular surname.

ngagement, and naval casualties were light.

ENEMY COMPLETELY SURPRISED

COMMANDOS LED BY LORD LOVAT

The Exchange Telegraph Company's special correspondent, who was on board a naval light craft, writes that complete surprise enabled the force of Commandos, led by Major Lord Lovat, to carry out their two-hour reconnaissance raid with negligible casualties.

The Germans, evidently not contemplating a landing, engaged the covering light force with German *flak* ships and smaller craft, and with the attention of the defences distracted, the Commandos swept across several hundred yards to the safety of the sand dunes at the top of the beach. They had gained the initiative and held it.

Veiled in light mist, the landing craft had crept silently inshore, and the Commandos had dropped swiftly and quietly into the shallows through which they had to wade to the beach. Searchlights began to flicker. The Nazi defenders, perhaps with memories of Bruneval and St. Nazaire, were showing signs of disquiet.

Whistles were sounded. They could be heard by the advancing troops, and, in the words of Lord Lovat, that was the moment when they " might have had to face withering machine-gun fire " as they raced to the sand dunes.

But the Commandos had swept across the sand and were at the beach wire before they

Above, how *The Times* of Thursday 23 April 1942 reported the raid on Hardelot.

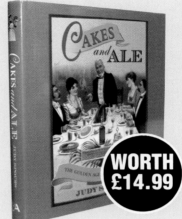

Book Reviews

Every month in *Ancestors* we include reviews of the latest family history books. Here are a selection of the most notable books we have read recently

COLLINS TRACING YOUR FAMILY HISTORY

Anthony Adolph

£20

ISBN 978-0-00-727492-0

Collins

In the first edition of this book – and the related volumes which followed – Anthony Adolph set a new standard for genealogy books. For the first time, a major publisher had really invested time, money and imagination in what was to become a bestseller. Now, four years later, comes a new edition which the cover claims to be "fully web-linked", whatever that means.

It remains a thorough and comprehensive guide to all the major, and many of the minor sources, although specialists may occasionally question statements made by the author. As you would wish, it is pretty up to date, for example it notes that the Family Records Centre has closed, and that the 1911 census will be released during 2009. In addition, there are interesting sections about using DNA, heraldry, and curiously, psychics. There is also an emphasis on the multi-cultural nature of modern British society with examples given of research by Black and Asian Britons.

GROW YOUR OWN FAMILY TREE

Alan Stewart

£16.99

ISBN 978-0-14051588-6

Penguin

It is a sign of how much family history has changed when a major new introduction to the subject largely concentrates on online resources. One of the great strengths of Alan Stewart's new book is that it is very web savvy.

The book is divided into 25 separate chapters covering most of the basic subjects. In part because of the author's Scottish antecedents, some of the strongest chapters are for Scotland and Ireland. This is welcome because in most such guides "the Celtic fringe" is normally relegated to a chapter at the end.

Inevitably there are errors and omissions. The section relating to the Family Records Centre is plain wrong and there is nothing about the various series of records relating to land ownership, such as the tithe and the Valuation Office plans and books.

THE FAMILY AND LOCAL HISTORY HANDBOOK

Robert and Elizabeth Blatchford

£9.99

ISBN 978-0-955239-91-5

Robert Blatchford Publishing Ltd

The 11th edition of this essential guide follows the format of previous editions with a variety of articles and a directory of useful addresses. The directory is the heart of the book and presumably, the real reason why people buy copies. Entries, in the main, have been fully updated and include family and local history societies, archives and libraries, cemeteries, and museums (including military and police) across the UK and on occasion, further afield. It is of course possible to find all this information online, but the Handbook may generally be more convenient. Indeed, the book as a whole benefits from a clearer and fresher design.

Most of the Handbook comprises articles by top family and local history writers. Between them they cover most of the basics – with guides, for example, to The National Archives, tracing Army ancestry and births, and marriages and deaths in Scotland. But there are many other pieces, some on fairly obscure topics, such as Regency Hull.

FAMILY HISTORY IN THE GENES:

Trace your DNA and grow your family tree

Chris Pomery

£7.99

ISBN 978-1-905615-12-4

The National Archives

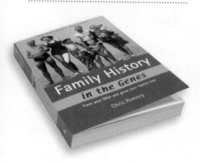

A few years ago family historians would have shaken their heads in amazement. But increasingly genealogists are taking DNA tests in the hope that the information will help them connect branches in the family tree.

But does this really help?

In this book Chris Pomery provides a clear answer, explaining what the results will and, as important, will not tell you about your ancestral origins, and provides excellent advice about finding a test company and the science behind the tests themselves. If you are thinking of having a test you should read this book before you do: you may save a lot of money and perhaps some grief.

He stresses that although tests for individuals are interesting, they are most useful as part of a study, perhaps one involving a particular surname and its variants. The author uses the Pomeroy study, with which he is involved, as an example throughout. Indeed there is a chapter about running or participating in such a project, together with details of the many projects which you can join.

If you want to know about the science behind the various tests available there are chapters which explain it in more detail. There is also a glossary explaining some of the terminology in more detail.

Often family history books can be turgid reads, with fact piling up upon fact with seemingly no explanation, but not in this case. Chris Pomery is a fine writer explaining what is frankly an extremely complicated subject very simply, but without patronising the reader. You won't find a better introduction to what is rapidly becoming a subject of great importance in the family history world.

FAMILY HISTORY IN THE WARS:

How your ancestors served their country

William Spencer

£7.99

ISBN 978-1-903365-95-3

The National Archives

Thanks to conscription and National Service, almost everyone has had a relative who served in the British armed forces during the 20th century. This small but densely packed book is an ideal introduction to the sources you will need to look at to reconstruct their service. It covers not only the three armed services but also looks at the Merchant Navy and some other forms of service such as the Home Guard, Special Operations Executive and the Women's Land Army.

The first part looks at the kind of things you might already have which will help in your search – when and where they served, whether you have any photographs, medals or documents – and how you can use them to get started. There is a useful "Operations Gazetteer" listing the various wars, both great and small, that our armed forces took part in up to the 1950s.

There are guides on where to find individual service documents, the records of the units they served with, and how to find details of their medals. In addition, he discusses resources for courts martial, casualties, civil defence and prisoners of war.

THE GREATEST GENEALOGY TIPS IN THE WORLD

Maureen Vincent-Northam

£6.99

ISBN 978-1-905151-72-1

The Greatest in the World Ltd

There are many books to get newcomers to family history up and running quickly. *The Greatest Genealogy Tips* distinguishes itself from the crowd by providing advice and an assortment of hints from the author's personal experiences. The book is primarily for family historians who have done some research, hit the proverbial brick wall, and are now wondering what the next step should be.

Vital guidance is included in shaded boxes and headed "Quick Tip"; random facts are included in bordered text boxes and headed "Did you know?"; and each chapter concludes with a bullet point summary.

However, this book does have certain shortcomings. The author's sometimes casual style leads to statements such as "A fire in Dublin in 1922 destroyed thousands of records, including the census returns from 1861 to 1891".

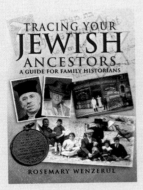

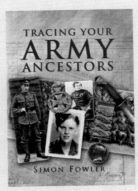
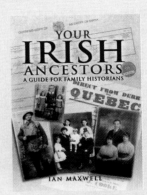

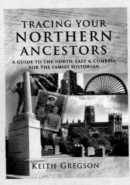
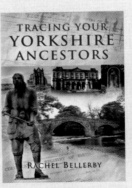
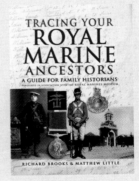

cd reviews

Ancestors magazine regularly reviews the latest CDs and here we include a selection of the latest releases.

Many resources have been published on CD by commercial companies, individuals and family history societies. They include street directories, parish registers and old reference books, all of which might be impossible to find elsewhere. They are easy to use, and it only takes a few seconds to find the names or places in which you are interested. Here are a selection of the latest releases.

Lists of names

The Medical Directory 1895 (S&N British Data Archive, £17.95) contains doctors in Great Britain, Ireland and India, with a further section on those resident abroad. In general, potted biographies are given only for those in London, which will indicate further sources for some lucky family historians to follow up, but even those whose ancestors worked outside the metropolis will find this a very useful resource. It also includes dentists licensed by the Royal College of Surgeons and miscellaneous organisations and regulatory bodies.

The first modern edition of *Who's Who* was published in 1897 in the format with which we are familiar today. **Who's Who 1897** (S&N £17.45) has entries for celebrities and worthies of the late Victorian period from Dan Leno to the Bishop of Dunedin.

Between the 1870s and the First World War, the journalist Edwin Walford edited a series of volumes with details of all the well-to-do families, particularly in rural areas. If families refused to co-operate in a gentle form of blackmail, he published details of their earnings. **County Families of the United Kingdom 1894** (S&N £17.95) is a survey of the people who ran the countryside at the height of late-Victorian confidence.

The happiest days of their lives

Founded in 1845, Marlborough College was intended for the sons of clergymen, and many of those listed in **Marlborough College**

Register 1843–1904 (S&N £17.45) did have a church background. As well as containing the standard lists of staff and pupils – with details of their parentage and careers, awards, prizes and sporting achievements – this publication details various associations to which Old Boys were connected. One is the Marlborough Mission in Tottenham, London, founded in 1881. Less worthy (but probably more fun), the Marlborough Nomads Football Club and the Marlborough Blues Cricket Club catered for the sporty types who wanted to go on playing after they had left the school.

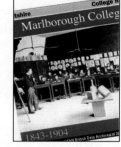

Eton was founded in 1440 to give poor but bright boys an education. The aristocracy, however, soon recognised this was too good a thing to leave entirely to the children of the working classes and started to send their own children there too. **Old Public School-Boys' Who's Who: Eton 1933** (S&N £17.45) shows just how many influential positions the Old Boys alive in 1933 held, from MPs to army officers to university dons, shaping the minds of future rulers.

Transcripts of records and indexes

Bristol and Avon Family History Society have put on disc more volumes of the **Bristol Diocese Marriage Registers: Groom and Bride Indexes & Transcripts.** Volume 9 covers 1754–1812, and Volume 11, 1837–1901. Registers from all parishes in the diocese are included. Each disc costs £9 (including p&p).

Nonconformist Baptismal Registers in Bristol Record Offices 1754 to 1827 (£9 including p&p) covers some registers from the major denominations – Methodist, Congregational, Presbyterian, Baptist, Society of Friends (Quaker) and Unitarian – in Bristol and Gloucestershire, along with a couple of lesser known ones – the Swedenborgian and Moravian churches. Usefully it also includes one Roman Catholic church in Bristol. The material is presented as a simple A–Z index of individuals, so all the researcher needs is the name of an ancestor – it isn't necessary to know to which

TOP TIP

Unless indicated, discs can be obtained from S&N Genealogy Supplies, West Wing, Manor Farm, Chilmark SP3 5AF; telephone 01722 716121; **www. genealogysupplies. com**. Please add £2.50 postage and packaging per order.

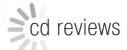

denomination his or her family belonged. Occupations and additional notes are also given.

In 1795 a map of all the properties in the town of Chipping Sodbury in Gloucestershire was produced to aid the setting of the Poor Law Rate. A branch of the Bristol & Avon FHS – the Sodbury Vale Family History Group – has been diligently tracing many of the owners, occupiers and trades that occupied buildings in the map, down to the present day. The result, published as **Butcher, Baker, Candle Maker: Chipping Sodbury from 1795** (£9 including p&p), provides a detailed history of the town and its businesses. It is arranged by individual building, sometimes photographed, with lists of inhabitants – drawn from census returns and trade directories – plus additional notes from other local history sources. The source of the information, which allows further research, is also included. There is also an accompanying 400 page book listing all property owners since 1795. Together with the CD this costs £20.50 (including p&p).

From: Bristol & Avon Family History Society, 3 Elm Tree Park, Sheepway, Portbury, Bristol BS20 7WW; **www.bafhs.org.uk**.

More registers appear on **Shropshire Nonconformist & Roman Catholic Registers 1657–1837** (Anguline, £8), which contains three volumes, originally privately printed in 1903 and 1913. The 22 Nonconformist congregations are divided into two parts and there is a third containing five Roman Catholic registers. As well as the transcripts, there are notes on the histories of individual churches and their ministers and congregations, including in some cases, the local opposition and even violence their presence provoked. The account books of some of the congregations add further insights into the lives of the worshippers. There seems to be no search facility by keyword but the publications are indexed.

Knaresborough Wills 1506–1858 (Anguline, £8) contains transcripts of wills (sometimes with inventories) and administrations from the Knaresborough Court Rolls 1506–1668. It also has an index of wills proved in the Prerogative Court of Canterbury between 1640 and 1858 relating to the Honour of Knaresborough, which was part of the Duchy of Lancaster, in Yorkshire. Originally published in 1902, when it was taken for granted that the average historian would have a knowledge of Latin and how ancient clerks abbreviated it, the early wills will need to be translated by an expert. The index to Somerset House wills (now at The National Archives) was

published in 1905 so does not include the modern reference numbers. However, there is enough information – name, date, occupation, place of residence – to point researchers in the right direction.

From: Anguline Research Archives, 51 Bank Street, Ossett WF5 8PR; **http://anguline.co.uk**.

An Index of Names mentioned in Wills proved at Carlisle Consistory Court 1727–1858: Vol. 1 1727–1778 (Cumbria Family History Society, £13.80 inc p&p) contains some 90,000 names of every person mentioned in the wills entered in the registers of the court. As the man who began the project, Trevor Littleton, notes, there are some differences between the original wills and the registers. He has also usefully added a few notes to enhance the information. The Index has to be installed on the computer rather than simply consulted. Volume 2 (1779–1820), containing a similar number of names, is in preparation and should be available soon.

From: Cumbria Family History Society T L Littleton, Rose Villa, 25 Eden Street, Carlisle, CA3 9LS, **www.cumbriafhs.com**.

Finding your way around
UK Maps Collection (S&N, two discs, £17.95) is a marvellous compilation of maps from across the country, mainly from the Victorian period, but ranging from London in 1660 to Leicestershire and Rutland in 1941. There are some county maps and others of single towns. In some cases there is more than one map of the same place at different times, enabling the user to see the development of an area. It seems easier to choose the size of the display using the percentage button rather than the zoom in/out facility to see each map in detail.

The superb **Finding your way round London in 1799** (Motco Enterprises, £22.50 inc p&p) contains the first edition of Richard Horwood's 26-inches-to-the-mile map of the London area, including the area south of the Thames. Clicking onto streets and subjects (like schools) in the indexes brings up the appropriate point on the map. Once reached, it can be enlarged or the map moved to show what else was in the vicinity. This is a wonderful resource for those with London ancestors enabling a virtual walk through the city they knew. It is one of a series of discs containing maps from various dates of the metropolis in the 18th and 19th centuries.

From: Motco Enterprises The Court House, Shamley Green Guildford GU5 0UB, **www.motco.com**.